Contents

Introduction

"Who do you say that I am?" This was the key question of Jesus' public ministry. He knew that people must recognize who He was before they could make a firm choice to follow Him as one of His disciples. So all through His ministry He did things and spoke words intended to present His credentials as Son of Man and Son of God, the world's only Saviour.

Most people today know little or nothing about Jesus. Even many Christians have much to learn from the Bible as to who Jesus is. True, these know Him personally as their Saviour through the experience of the new birth. But because they have never thoroughly and systematically studied all four gospels, they have yet to hear God's full introduction of His Son to the world.

Any study of the full scope of Christ's life must make a comparative analysis of all four gospels, especially to see the chronological order of events in Jesus' career and to make full topical studies of aspects of that career. Hence this manual in the Bible Self-Study Series. It goes without saying that the merits of studying each gospel separately, in the form in which God originally gave them to the world, are manifold. Other books in this series treat the gospels thus, separately.

If the reader has never accepted Christ as his personal Saviour, it is sincerely hoped that such an experience will be the fruit of this study of Christ's life. For the Christian reader who has not as yet made an organized study of the life of Christ by comparing all four gospels, and intends now to do so, many blessings are in store as he begins to learn new and marvelous truths about his Lord. I have had mainly the Christian in mind in writing this book.

LIFE OF CHRIST
A SELF-STUDY GUIDE

Irving L. Jensen

MOODY PRESS
CHICAGO

Suggestions for study

This study manual is written to encourage independent study by the reader. The Bible is everyman's book, composed in such a manner that the average reader can comprehend its important truths for his personal light and inspiration. No greater thrill and satisfaction can come to the Bible student than to discover Bible truths himself.

Outside study aids should supplement, not supplant, independent Bible study. In addition to encouraging independent study, this manual serves as a supplementary aid to that study. There is little of commentary in the manual.[1] Rather, questions and suggestions abound. Also, I have included a number of charts and outlines to help the reader maintain his bearing on the ocean of facts recorded in the gospels. Visual charts are valuable "eye gates" to new horizons.

Two of the most valuable clues to the meaning of the Bible passage that one is studying are:

1. Seeing the *relations* of things: How is one individual fact related to another fact and to the whole story?

2. Recognizing *emphasized* truths: What is primary, and what is subordinate, in the biblical account?

The lessons of this manual keep reminding the reader to look for these clues in his study.

The reader may wish to use a harmony of the gospels as he proceeds with his study, in order to see the Bible text written in parallel columns whenever more than one gospel records the same event. The Bibliography lists some available harmonies.[2]

In choosing how long a unit should be studied at any one time, the student should recognize his own individual situation. Sometimes one entire lesson of this manual may be one study unit. Some lessons, because of the large amount of biblical text involved, should be divided into various study units.

1. I recommend highly the commentary aid of C.F. Pfeiffer and E.F. Harrison, eds., *The Wycliffe Bible Commentary* (Chicago: Moody, 1962). Other sources of help include the following volumes published by Moody Press: Merrill F. Unger, *The New Unger's Bible Handbook* (1966, 1984), and *The New Unger's Bible Dictionary* (1957, 1961, 1966, 1988); Charles F. Pfeiffer and Howard F. Vos, *The Wycliffe Historical Geography of Bible Lands* (1967). The last-named book gives excellent background to the story of Christ's life.
2. Generally, the chronological order of events in Jesus' life presented in this manual follows that of these two harmonies: A.T. Robertson, *A Harmony of the Gospels for Students of the Life of Christ* (New York: Harper, 1922); and Albert Cassel Wieand, *A New Harmony of the Gospels*, rev. ed. (Grand Rapids: Eerdmans, 1950).

Most of this manual is devoted to the period of time called Christ's public ministry. Other subjects, such as His present ministry, are important, but are treated only briefly for the obvious reason of limited space. These aspects of Christ's life may be studied more fully using other books of this series.

Here are further study reminders applicable to all Bible study:

1. Seek *first* to learn what the Bible says. This is the step of Observation. Never tire of examining carefully the Bible text. Look, look, look! ("The hearing ear, and *the seeing eye* the Lord hath made even both of them," Prov. 20:12.) Then try to determine what the passage means (Interpretation). Finally, seek the intended Application.

2. In using this manual, observe the directions to read all Bible passages cited. Remember that your *basic* study is of the *Bible* text, not of any commentary or study guide.

3. Always have pencil and paper next to your Bible as you study. "The pencil is one of the best eyes." It will surprise you how many new vistas appear once you begin to record your observations.

4. If you are a Christian, the Holy Spirit, who inspired the Scriptures, indwells your spirit and offers illumination to discern the intent of the spiritual truths of the Bible. There is no better teacher of spiritual truths than the Holy Spirit.

5. Never fail to apply the Bible to your own life. The natural tendency is to apply it to others. Others are involved, but seek to find a personal application in the passage you are studying. As you examine the words God has chosen to include in the four gospels, may your vision of Christ be so enlarged and sharpened that your life will be different. A serious study venture in the subject The Life of Christ must inevitably bring about such an experience, to the glory of God.

Suggestion to leaders in group study:

If you are leading a group in Bible study, here are some suggestions:

1. Tell group members what they should study before coming together to discuss the lesson. Encourage faithful completion of homework, including answering of questions in the manual.

2. Don't lecture. As you teach, encourage the group to ask questions and to offer comments. Plan definitely to use the latter part of your time together in discussion. Encourage everyone to participate. Honor all questions, simple or difficult, whether you

are able to give a satisfactory answer or not. Let others offer answers as well.

3. Construct a large copy of Chart J: The Earthly Life of Christ, and hang this in a prominent place for all your meetings. This will be a constant reminder of where you are in the story of Jesus' life.

4. The first part of each meeting should be devoted to a review of the previous lesson. In the last part of the meeting summarize the lesson and encourage ways to apply the truths learned.

5. Be a good leader in setting an atmosphere conducive to learning more about Christ. Let there be a deep conviction of the truth and authority of God's Word and a dependency on Him for help in understanding it.

> Let us now go . . . and see this thing
> which is come to pass. (Luke 2:15*b*)

Lesson 1
Before the Event of Bethlehem

The thirty-three-year span of Christ's earthly biography is small as compared to the subject of His total life. There were antecedents leading up to His birth, and sequels since His death and resurrection are still shaping world history. Before we begin study of the events of Jesus' earthly life, it would be enlightening to consider some subjects that are related to His life in an anticipatory way.

I. THE PREINCARNATE CHRIST

The birth of Jesus in Bethlehem was the first event of His earthly career as the incarnate ("in the flesh") Son of God. But He existed before that time. For Christ, like the Father and the Spirit, did not have a beginning—He has always existed. When John says (referring to Jesus) that the Word was "in the beginning" (John 1:1), he is simply declaring that when creation's time began its course (Gen. 1:1), the Word, or Jesus, was already existing.

The Bible does not furnish many specific details about the preincarnate Christ, or, for that matter, about the ascended Lord. That which it does tell us is vital to know. Study Chart A, then read each Bible reference shown. Record in a few words the essence of each verse. (You may recall other verses that apply to this survey.) What are the important truths that the Bible teaches about the preincarnate Christ?

_____

_____

_____

ETERNITY PAST	ETERNITY FUTURE
HE EXISTED BEFORE THE CREATION of the UNIVERSE.	Heb. 13:8
John 1:1	Rev. 11:15
8:57-58 (cf. Phil. 2:6)	
17:5	**NEW CREATION**
Eph. 1:4	Rev. 21:1 (cf. 2 Pet. 3:11-12)
ORIGINAL CREATION	
He, with the Father and Holy Spirit, created the universe and has been sustaining it.	
John 1:3; 1 Cor. 8:6	**MILLENNIAL AGE**
Eph. 3:9; Col. 1:15-16*	Rev. 20:1-6
Col. 1:17; Heb. 1:2, 10	
OLD TESTAMENT DAYS	
He worked in O.T. times in the lives of believers.	**CHURCH AGE**
—as "angel of Jehovah" Judges 6:11-23; 1 Kings 19:5-7	Heb. 4:14-16
—as "Jehovah" Gen. 19:24; Hos. 1:7	John 14:2-3
—as "Word" John 1:1-5	

BIRTH of JESUS	ASCENSION of JESUS
HE CAME DOWN—glory surrendered Phil. 2:5-8	glory restored—HE WENT UP Phil. 2:9-11

EARTHLY LIFE OF JESUS

* Some translators translate "primeval Creator" instead of "firstborn."

How is this doctrine related to that of His deity?

_____

_____

Make a special study of Christ's humiliation (from throne to cross) in Philippians 2:5-8; and of Christ's exaltation (from cross to throne) in Philippians 2:9-11. What is the practical exhortation in this passage?

_____

_____

_____

II. THE ANCESTORS OF JESUS

Divine design in the ancestral line of a person is supremely manifested in the ancestry of Jesus. Every prophetic word uttered concerning Him in the centuries before He was born was spoken according to a perfect divine plan and fulfilled with the same accuracy. Of the things prophesied of Him, four were prominent:

1. He was to be of the human race (Isa. 9:6*a*).
2. He was to be of the messianic covenant line (Gen. 22:18; 49:10).
3. He was to be of the royal line of David (2 Sam. 7:14, 16; Isa. 11:1).
4. He was to be "The mighty God" (Isa. 9:6).

The two New Testament genealogies of Jesus (Matt. 1:1-17; Luke 3:23-38) bring out the above four fulfillments. To acquaint yourself with these genealogies, read the two lists and note the likenesses and differences. You may want to record the two lists in parallel columns to help you compare the two. (Record both in the advancing order of Matthew's.)

Chart B shows the prominent features of the two lists. Both genealogies are of Jesus, Luke giving the ancestors of Jesus' mother, Mary, and Matthew giving those of Jesus' legal father, Joseph.

Some observations:

1. How far back in the human race does each genealogy go?

_____

10

Luke's list gives the physical descent of Jesus,
     which could only be through Mary (Jesus being physically conceived
     of the Holy Spirit, not of Joseph).
     This is Mary's genealogy.

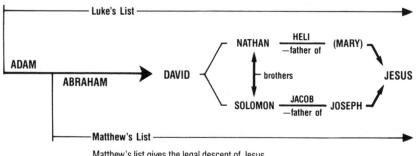

Matthew's list gives the legal descent of Jesus,
     which could only be through the male, Joseph.
     This is Joseph's genealogy.

Account for the difference, keeping in mind that Matthew wrote
especially with the Jew in mind.

_____

_____

2. Compare the lists from Abraham to David.

_____

_____

3. Note that the brothers Nathan and Solomon were the forefa-
thers, respectively, of Heli (father of Mary) and Jacob (father of Joseph). Which brother succeeded David on the throne? (cf. 1 Kings
1:13).

_____

4. Matthew divides his list into three groups (rounded off to fourteen generations each for convenience): Abraham to David (the-
ocracy); David to Babylon (monarchy); Babylon to Christ (hierar-
chy). Was Israel's history generally bright or dark during these
periods?

_____

5. Matthew uses the word "begat," which in Jewish genealogies usually referred to a son but sometimes referred to even more dis-

11

tant offspring, such as a grandson. For example, Matthew 1:8 says, "Joram begat Ozias," but 1 Chronicles 3:11-12 indicates that there were three descendants of Joram before Ozias was born. Such genealogical "gaps" are not errors in the Bible but rather allowable liberties that the recorders took for the purpose of the record.

Now let us see how the genealogy of Jesus fulfilled the four prophecies listed earlier in this section.

1. *Son of Man.* Jesus was identified literally with the human race, born in human flesh (cf. Gal. 4:4). Luke emphasizes His identity with the entire human race by going back to the first man, Adam. Matthew brings out the "human" aspect of this race (though Jesus was not bound by any limitations of humanity) by citing names with moral blots (e.g., Rahab) and by making a big point of the captivity of Judah in Babylon.

2. *Messiah.* Four times in the first eighteen verses of Matthew Jesus is indentified as the Christ (the word is from the Greek *chrio*, "anoint"), a title equivalent to Messiah. Matthew also emphasizes this messianic aspect in the opening statement, identifying Jesus as the "son of Abraham" (1:1). Also, Matthew's list of names begins with Abraham. It was with Abraham that God first made His covenant with Israel, promising them everlasting blessing (cf. Gen. 12:2-3; 17:3-8). Jesus came to be not only the hope of the world but also the deliverer of Israel.

3. *King.* Matthew calls Jesus "the son of David" (1:1). He repeats the phrase "David the king" twice in 1:6. The royal line of David, continued through Solomon his heir, is recorded by Matthew. It is noteworthy that the bloodline of Jesus (Mary's descent), recorded by Luke, also reaches back to David.

4. *Son of God.* Both genealogies are careful to guard the truth of Jesus' deity, His birth being of supernatural conception by the Holy Spirit (cf. Matt. 1:20). Joseph was Jesus' legal father only. Matthew says that Joseph was "the husband of Mary, of whom was born Jesus"(Matt. 1:16). The phrase "of whom" is in the feminine form in Greek, referring only to Mary. Note how, a few verses later (v. 23), Matthew explicitly identifies Jesus as God.

The reading of Luke 3:23 also guards the truth that Jesus was conceived of the Holy Spirit, not of Joseph. The verse literally reads, "And Jesus . . . being (as was supposed, son of Joseph),[1] of

---

1. The closing parenthesis placed here can be justified by the original Greek and also makes more sense. See A.T. Robertson, *A Harmony of the Gospels for Students of the Life of Christ* (New York: Harper, 1922), p. 261. Compare the Berkeley version of this verse.

PROPHECY	DESCRIPTION	FULFILLMENT
	PRE-EXISTENCE AND BIRTH	
Isa. 11:1		Rev. 22:16
Isa. 7:14		Matt. 1:18-23
Mic. 5:2		Matt. 2:1; Luke 2:1-7
Dan. 9:25		Luke 3:1, 21-22
	PUBLIC MINISTRY	
Mal. 3:1; 4:5-6 Isa. 40:3-4		Luke 1:13-17; Matt. 3:1-3, 16; 17:10-13
Isa. 11:2		Matt. 3:16
Isa. 61:1-3		Luke 4:16-21
Isa. 53:3		Mark 3:6
Zech. 9:9		Matt. 21:1-11
	DEATH AND RESURRECTION	
Isa. 53:4-8; Dan. 9:26		John 19:18; 2 Cor. 5:21; 1 Pet. 3:18
Ps. 34:20; Ex. 12:46		John 19:33, 36
Zech. 13:7		Matt. 26:31, 56
Isa. 53:9, 12		Luke 23:32-33; Matt. 27:57-60; John 19:39
Ps. 22:7-8		Matt. 27:39-43
Ps. 22:18		Matt. 27:35; John 19:23-24
Ps. 22:1		Matt. 27:46; Mark 15:34
Ps. 16:10; Isa. 53:10		Matt. 28:1-6; Acts 2:22-32
	PRESENT AND FUTURE MINISTRIES	
Ps. 110:1, 4		Acts 5:31; Heb. 8:1
Isa. 9:6-7; Dan. 7:13-14		Luke 1:32-35; Matt. 25:31

Heli." Heli was Mary's father and thus was Jesus' grandfather. So Luke's list begins with the recognition of the supernatural virgin birth of the Son of God. (Observe that Luke ends the list with a reference to the divine creation of the father of the human race, Adam, "of God" [Luke 3:38].)

It is interesting to observe that two gospels, Mark and John, identify Jesus as God in the very first verses. Mark 1:1 records the grand genealogical fact: "Jesus Christ, the Son of God." John 1:1 says clearly, "The Word was God."

III. PROPHECIES FULFILLED IN JESUS

Over and over the Old Testament Scriptures pointed to Christ as the coming One. Hundreds of such prophecies are in the indirect form of types, such as offerings, feasts, events, institutions, men, the Tabernacle and its articles. More than three hundred prophecies are stated directly in words, relating to some aspect of Christ's Person or work. A familiar expression in the gospels, appearing about thirty-five times, is "that it might be fulfilled," referring back to an Old Testament prophecy. Everything about Jesus was in accord with a divine plan, drawn before the foundation of the world.

The accompanying list in Chart C gives the locations of some of the major messianic prophecies and their fulfillments. Look up each verse, and record in the middle column a brief description of the prophecy.

IV. THE WORLD INTO WHICH JESUS CAME

"When the fulness of the time was come, God sent forth his Son . . ." (Gal. 4:4). The time was right as to preparation, for the law had served its disciplinary and instructive purposes. The time was right also as to political, religious, and social climate, conducive to the ministry of the gospel; and it was right as to need—a spiritual vacuum was waiting to be filled.

The world of Jesus' day was ruled by Gentile Rome. The particular people to whom He primarily ministered were the Jews of Palestine. (Read Matt. 15:24.) Chart D is a summary tabulation intended to describe these two "worlds" of Jesus' day, Gentile and Jewish.

This is James Stalker's description of the Jewish world to which Jesus came:

> A nation enslaved; the upper classes devoting themselves to self-ishness, courtiership, and skepticism; the teachers and chief professors of religion lost in mere shows of ceremonialism, and

ROMAN EMPIRE	JEWISH PEOPLE
POLITICAL SETTING	
—Unification of the Mediterranean world —Safe and easy communication —Universal language —Universal peace	—Under the yoke of Rome —Expectation of a Deliverer, of their own race —Sanhedrin (the Jewish organ of local government) had only limited power
MORAL SETTING	
—Degradation —"To corrupt and be corrupt is the spirit of the times" (Tacitus)	—Generally strict standards —Sadducees sponsored moral compromise
INTELLECTUAL SETTING	
—Greek and Roman culture highly developed	—Education a prominent part of the Jews' life
RELIGIOUS SETTING	

—Heathen idolatry
 	
—Mystic religions
 	
—Philosophic religions
 	
—Spiritual vacuum
	—Generally intensely religious as to externals
	—Religious life molded by three sects:
	  1. Pharisees: rigid legalists; self-righteous; middle class
	  2. Sadducees: free thinkers; worldly; upper class
	  3. Essenes: mystic pietists; ascetics
	—Synagogues and rabbis: a thriving institution of worship, which arose after the exile
	—A believing remnant: there were some who looked and prayed for the advent of the Messiah (read Luke 2:21-39)

boasting themselves the favorites of God, while their souls were honeycombed with self-deception and vice; the body of the people misled by false ideals; and seething at the bottom of society, a neglected mass of unblushing and unrestrained sin.[2]

Concerning the Graeco-Roman world of Jesus' day, G.T. Manley writes:

> We must not, of course, exaggerate the preparedness of the Graeco Roman world for the acceptance of Christianity. It needed three centuries of intensive evangelization and heroic witness-bearing to overcome the pride and self-satisfaction begot-

2. James Stalker, *The Life of Jesus Christ* (Westwood, N.J.: Revell, 1880), pp. 35-36.

ten of so mighty and dazzling a civilization. But its external order, its deep spiritual aspirations, and its groping after truth, all assured the presence in it of good soil when the Sower came with His seed which is the word of God.[3]

V. CONCLUDING EXERCISES

Compare the world today with the world of Jesus' day, with respect to the need for the gospel and the opportunities of its proclamation. How is the gospel relevant to the life of man today? Is the gospel for *all* peopled?

Jesus is coming again. Will the event be as real as His first coming? Read John 14:1-3; 1 Thessalonians 4:16-18. Then read Luke 2:21-32 again, and observe that Simeon was waiting for the coming of the Messiah *while* he was *serving* in the Temple. Try to recall passages in the New Testament that exhort the believer to *wait* and *work* until the coming of the Lord.

3. G.T. Manley, ed., *The New Bible Handbook* (Chicago: InterVarsity, 1947), p. 293.

Lesson 2
The Gospels'
Four Portraits of Jesus

The biography of Jesus is written in four separate books in the Bible, composed by four different authors. It is clear that God had good reasons for His design of four separate gospel records in the Bible's canon, rather than one book. The Bible does not tell us what those reasons are, though one suggestion is made by Luke in Luke 1:1-4. But a comparison of the gospels reveals at least five purposes of the fourfold format:

I. CONTENT

This is the prime reason for four gospels. For example, four different portraits of Jesus, taken from different angles, with different background and lighting, are shown. This would not be possible with just one biography. Other subjects concerning the life of Christ and the gospel He preached (shown on Chart E) can be treated in the same way. "We spend more time, and ... feel more at home, in the four successive chambers than we should have done in one long gallery."[1]

II. CONTACT

This is another important reason for four gospels. The three main groups of people to be reached, culturewise, were the Jews, the Romans, and the Greeks. Matthew, Mark, and Luke wrote their gospels with these people in mind, respectively. John's gospel crosses all the culture lines and has the universal church in mind.

---

1. Thomas Bernard, *The Progress of Doctrine In The New Testament* (Grand Rapids: Eerdmans, 1949), p. 59.

III. CLARITY

Each gospel is a complement to the other three, so that what may appear unclear or incomplete in one gospel is clarified and brought into focus by comparing the others.

IV. CONFIRMATION

The impact of four independent witnesses to the same facts is impressive, especially in view of the different yet noncontradictory reports that are given of the same events.

V. COPIOUS BULK

If one account had been written to include the material of the four gospels without duplication, that single gospel would have been considerably shorter than the present four gospels. Bulkwise, the

COMPARISONS OF THE FOUR GOSPELS CHART E

	MATTHEW	MARK	LUKE	JOHN
Portraits of Jesus	The Prophesied King	The Obedient Servant	The Perfect Man	The Divine Son
Prominent words	"fulfilled"	"straightway"	"Son of man"	"believe"
Cultures of the original readers	Jews (Jesus, Son of (Abraham)	Romans (Action: no genealogy)	Greeks (Jesus, Son of Adam)	Church (Jesus, Son of God)
Outlook and style of the writers	Teacher	Preacher	Litterateur	Theologian
Outstanding sections	Sermons	Miracles	Parables	Doctrines
Prominent ideas	Law	Power	Grace	Glory
Broad division	"SYNOPTIC GOSPELS" —stressing the humanity of Christ, from the outward, earthly side			"FOURTH GOSPEL" —stressing the deity of Christ, from the inward, heavenly side

gospels make up about half of the New Testament. The intended
emphasis of the gospel story is reiterated by the very space devoted to it.

Chart E is a tabulation of the various ways in which the gospels may be compared. Included are comparisons of content,
original readers, authors, and style.

VI. EXERCISE

You will find the exercise of analysis in Chart F to be an interesting and fruitful study. Compare the four pictures of Christ as He is

FOUR PICTURES OF CHRIST　　　　　　　　　　　　　　　　　　**Chart F**

MATT. 28:18-20
ROYAL LAWGIVER

MARK 16:16-20
MIGHTY WORKER

AUTHORITY

18
Jesus said:
ALL AUTHORITY in heaven — to
on earth — me

JESUS'
ABSOLUTE
AUTHORITY

16

ORDINANCE

LAWS

Go therefore
MAKE DISCIPLES

BAPTIZING in name — Father
of — Son
TEACHING . . . — Holy Spirit

all that I have COMMANDED YOU

I am with you ALWAYS
20

JESUS'
CONTINUING
PRESENCE

20

LUKE 24:50-53
FRIEND OF MAN

JOHN 20:28-31
SON OF GOD

50

52

53

28

31

19

portrayed in the concluding words of each gospel. (The passage of John shown below is the last part of the gospel, appearing before the epilogue.) Record key words and phrases of the biblical text in the boxes, and record your own outlines in the margins. A title for each passage is suggested as a starter. The passage of Matthew is completed as an example.

Lesson 3
The Geography of Jesus' Public Ministry

The main ingredients of history are people, places, things, and events—all prominent in Scripture. The second ingredient, places, is the subject of geography. The geography of Jesus' public ministry is an important area for study since His frequent travels through the land of Palestine reveal much about the extent and character of His purposes and goals. Also, an acquaintance with its geography makes any biography come alive and helps the student visualize the action and retain it in his memory. Let your study of this lesson become that fruitful for you.

It is the purpose of this lesson to introduce the most important features of the geography of Jesus' career. You will find it helpful to refer to a more detailed map of Palestine as you proceed with the lesson.

I. PHYSICAL FEATURES OF PALESTINE

The physical features (e.g., terrain and bodies of water) determine where cities and villages spring up. In Palestine, six regions run from the north to the south, each with its own distinctive physical features. These are shown on the map on Chart G.

A. Observations

1. The Shefelah region contains the gradually rising hills from the coastal plain to the Cis-Jordan hills, also called the Judean hills. The average elevation of these is 2,000 feet.

2. Most of the cities of Christ's ministry lie along the Cis-Jordan hills and around the Sea of Galilee.

3. The two major north-south travel routes were along the Cis-Jordan Range and the Jordan Valley. The entire Jordan Valley is below sea level.

21

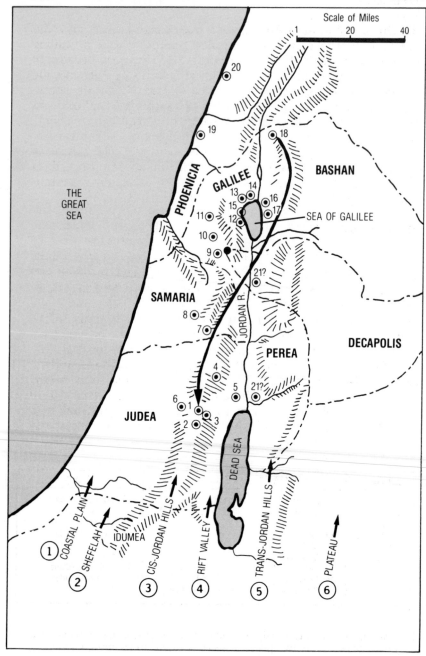

II. CLIMATE

The climate of most of Palestine has not changed much since the days of Jesus. That climate is controlled generally by the prevailing westerly winds from the Mediterranean Sea. However, because of the varied configuration of the physical features of Palestine, the climate varies considerably from place to place. Generally speaking, there are two seasons: warm and dry summers, and mild and wet winters. The rainy season lasts from November to March. Average temperatures for Jerusalem, representing recent records, are 41 to 54 F. in January and 65 to 85 F. in August. The climate of Galilee, where Jesus lived most of His life and accomplished most of His public ministry, was more pleasant in the summer months than that of Judea and the south Jordan Valley.

III. CITIES AND VILLAGES

The cities and villages named in the gospels were located mainly in the three provinces of Judea, Samaria, and Galilee. Three surrounding areas were Perea, Decapolis, and Phoenicia. Locate these sections on Chart G.

After about a year of limited service in Judea in Jesus' public ministry, most of His itinerant work was done in and around Galilee, though His trips from Jerusalem to Galilee afforded many opportunities of ministry along the way. Of the many cities and villages that He visited on His evangelistic tours, only about twenty are mentioned by name in the gospels. Learning the locations of these places will help your study of the life of Christ. See how many locations you can spot on Chart G before referring to the following number key.

JUDEA	SAMARIA[1] AND GALILEE		OTHER
1. Jerusalem	7. Sychar		16. Bethsaida (Julias)
2. Bethlehem	8. Samaria		(Luke 9:10)
3. Bethany	9. Nain		17. Gergesa
4. Ephraim	10. Nazareth		18. Caesarea Philippi
5. Jericho	11. Cana		19. Tyre
6. Emmaus	12. Magdala		20. Sideon
	13. Capernaum		21. Bethabara (Bethany
	14. Chorazin	(Mark 6:45)	beyond Jordan)
	15. Bethsaida	(west side of Sea of Galilee)	

1. Travel in Samaria was usually avoided by Jews because of the religious antagonism between the two peoples. Jesus, however, freely moved about and ministered in Samaria. (Cf. John 4:4.)

Below are listed some verses that record parts of Jesus' itineraries. Check the context of each verse in your Bible, and then try to visualize the trip, either by foot or donkey, over the route involved. Record the geography involved.

Luke 10:30

Matt. 21:17

John 11:54

John 4:5

Luke 7:11

Luke 4:16

John 4:46

Matt. 4:13

Luke 9:10

Mark 8:27

Mark 7:24

John 1:28

IV. POLITICAL REGIONS

During Jesus' life the governing of Palestine was parcelled out among various rulers, all of them directly or indirectly responsible to Rome. Chart H lists the rulers, their domain, and dates.

TERRITORIES	RULERS			
			PROCURATORS	
JUDEA AND SAMARIA	HEROD the GREAT (43–4 B.C.)	ARCHE-LAUS (4 B.C.–A.D. 6)	Coponius Ambivius Rufus Gratus	PONTIUS PILATE (A.D. 26–36)
GALILEE AND PEREA	HEROD ANTIPAS (4 B.C.–A.D. 39) (Killed John the Baptist)			
ITUREA AND TRACHONITIS (northeast of Sea of Galilee)	PHILIP (4 B.C.–A.D. 34)			

Notes:

1. Herod the Great died in 4 B.C., not long after Jesus was born.[2] (Cf. Matt. 2:1, 19.)

2. Archelaus was the ruler whom Joseph avoided on arriving in Palestine from Egypt (Matt. 2:22).

3. Pontius Pilate was the Roman procurator of Judea during Jesus' public ministry (Luke 3:1), who officially condemned Jesus to death.

V. CONCLUDING EXERCISE

Why do you think Jesus ministered mainly in Galilee?

_____

_____

Compare this fact with the commission He gave to the apostles in Acts 1:8: "Ye shall be witnesses unto me both in Jerusalem, and in all Judea, and in Samaria, and unto the uttermost part of the earth."

2. Jesus was born around 5 or 6 B.C. It is an acknowleged fact that our present calendars are in error by a few years. See A. T. Robertson, *A Harmony of the Gospels for Students of the Life of Christ* (New York: Harper, 1922), pages 262-67, for a discussion of this.

Lesson 4
Jesus the God-Man

When Jesus walked this earth He could not have done what He did unless He had been who He was. When Jesus came to the peak and turning point of His preaching and sign-working ministry the great question He asked was a question of identification: "Who do men say that I am?" (Mark 8:27).

The Person of Christ is basic to the work of Christ. Before we proceed in the next chapters to our study of the life and ministry of Jesus, it will be of great help to see first who this Preacher and Teacher and Miracle Worker was.

I. THE TWO NATURES

The gospels do not present Jesus as two persons. He is always one Person, but with two natures. He is of divine nature, and He is of human nature. It is interesting to see how these two are brought together in the identification question quoted above and its answer. Matthew records the longer question, "Whom do men say that I the Son of man am?" (Matt. 16:13). The words "Son of man" refer to His human nature. When Peter told Jesus who he believed Jesus to be, he recognized Jesus' deity. "Thou art the Christ, the Son of the living God" (Matt.16:16).

Read the passages cited below to see how clear the Scriptures are in identifying the two natures of Jesus, divine and human. Record the main truth of each verse in the spaces afforded.

II. THE INDISSOLUBLE UNION

Thus Jesus has two natures: a real and true divine nature, and a real and true human nature. The other important doctrine related to this is that these two natures are indissolubly united in the one Person. Jesus is no less God because of His humanity and no less

26

Chart I

DIVINE	HUMAN
Identification with the Father (coeternal existence) "GOD . . .	Identification with the human race (incarnation) manifest in the FLESH" 1 Tim. 3:16

DIVINE	HUMAN
Divine Names John 1:1 John 10:36 Isa. 9:6 Matt. 1:23 John 20:28 Rev. 3:14 Rev. 22:13	**Human Names** Matt. 1:25 Matt. 1:1 Luke 9:22
	Human Nature Matt. 26:38 Matt. 26:26 Luke 24:39
Divine Attributes Heb. 1:11 Matt. 18:20 Col. 2:3 Heb. 1:3 Heb. 13:8	**Human Development** Gal. 4:4 Luke 2:40 Luke 2:52
Divine Works Mark 2:7 Mark 4:39 Mark 5:29 John 1:3 Col. 1:17 Matt. 16:27	**Human Wants and Emotions** Matt. 4:2 John 4:6 John 11:35 John 12:27 Heb. 5:7-8 Luke 22:44

human because of His deity. Each nature resides with the other, and both make up His personality. Jesus is not God and man; Jesus is God-man.

III. THE NECESSITY OF THE UNION

We cannot fully understand how Jesus is both truly divine and truly human at the same time, yet we can recognize the necessity of such a union if Jesus' work is of its intended and declared worth. Consider, for example, the following three ministries of Jesus:

A. Perfect Sacrifice

Only Jesus as God-man could offer to the Father a perfect substitutionary atoning sacrifice for man's sin.

B. Effective Priesthood

Only as God-man can He be the effective High Priest that He is, "seeing he ever liveth to make intercession" for those that come unto the Father by Him (Heb. 7:25).

C. Eternal Kingship

Only as God-man, slain for us, is He worthy of an eternal kingship, receiving "power, and riches, and wisdom, and strength, and honour, and glory, and blessing" (Rev. 5:12).

Thus we see that the crucial work of Christ is dependent on His being the true God-man.

IV. CONCLUSION

The Jesus of the gospels was the Son of God and the Son of man. What inspiration and assurance and comfort is ours now to know that He is the same today as He was then (Heb. 13:8). We cannot fully understand the doctrine of His Person, but we can know and love the Person Himself.

> Jesus Christ has trod the world.
> The trace of the Divine footsteps will never be obliterated.
> And the Divine footsteps were the footsteps of a Man.
> The example of Christ is such as men can follow.
> (Peter Bayne)

28

Lesson 5
Life of Christ: A Survey

We move now to the core of our study—an examination of the life and ministry of Christ. We will follow the correct order of study by first viewing Jesus' life as a whole and then analyzing the various periods. This lesson is a story of the life of Christ.

When the four gospels are brought together into one narrative, or harmony, a picture of Christ's life emerges that shows every important aspect of His redemptive career. Not every detail of Jesus' life is recorded (John 21:25), but nothing has been omitted that would serve a purpose in the divinely designed biblical portrait.

As recorded by the gospels, the life of Jesus was of three different and quantitatively unequal parts:

1. *Preparation* years, relatively obscure, about thirty years.
2. *Public ministry,* the highlights recorded in detail, about three and one-half years.
3. *Sacrifice,* the crucial events of Jesus' ministry transpiring over a period of only a few weeks. Chart J shows the periods and movements of Jesus' career. Study the chart carefully.

I. OBSERVATIONS

1. Mention was made above of *three* periods of Jesus' life: preparation, public ministry, *sacrifice.* Notice by Chart J the two phases of Jesus' life: to minister (serve) and to die. Observe that the peak of His public ministry was reached at least a year before His death. His death was *the* crucial event.

2. Jesus' public ministry lasted for about three and one-half years. The annual Passovers mentioned in John[1] are datelines that indicate this duration. Without John's gospel, which alone records

---

1. This study guide takes the position that the unnamed feast of John 5:1 was a Passover feast.

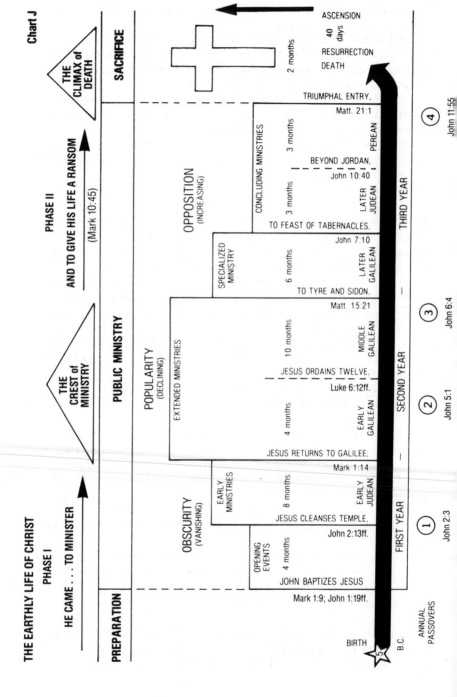

THE EARTHLY LIFE OF CHRIST

Chart J

PHASE I
HE CAME . . . TO MINISTER

PHASE II
AND TO GIVE HIS LIFE A RANSOM
(Mark 10:45)

| PREPARATION | PUBLIC MINISTRY | SACRIFICE |

THE CREST of MINISTRY

THE CLIMAX of DEATH

OBSCURITY (VANISHING)

POPULARITY (DECLINING)

OPPOSITION (INCREASING)

ASCENSION
40 days
RESURRECTION
DEATH
2 months

TRIUMPHAL ENTRY,
Matt. 21:1

CONCLUDING MINISTRIES
3 months
PEREAN

BEYOND JORDAN,
John 10:40
3 months
LATER JUDEAN

TO FEAST OF TABERNACLES,
John 7:10

SPECIALIZED MINISTRY
6 months
LATER GALILEAN

TO TYRE AND SIDON,
Matt. 15:21

EXTENDED MINISTRIES
10 months
MIDDLE GALILEAN

JESUS ORDAINS TWELVE,
Luke 6:12ff.

4 months
EARLY GALILEAN

JESUS RETURNS TO GALILEE,
Mark 1:14

EARLY MINISTRIES
8 months
EARLY JUDEAN

JESUS CLEANSES TEMPLE,
John 2:13ff.

OPENING EVENTS
4 months

JOHN BAPTIZES JESUS
Mark 1:9; John 1:19ff.

BIRTH

FIRST YEAR   SECOND YEAR   THIRD YEAR

① John 2:3   ② John 5:1   ③ John 6:4   ④ John 11:55

B.C.

ANNUAL PASSOVERS

30

4. The highest box on the chart represents the main core of Jesus' ministries—His *extended* ministries. Before this, there were the opening events; then the early ministries of the Early Judean period. When Jesus had completed His extended ministries, He turned His face and His footsteps toward Jerusalem, engaging in specialized and concluding ministries on His way to the cross.

5. The extended ministries of Jesus were performed in Galilee. Most of His services were rendered in this northern province, the land of His youth and young manhood. Note the other geographical regions of ministry.

6. Read the references cited in Chart J at the beginning of each new period of Jesus' ministry. These events are signposts of junctions in Jesus' career.

II. PRACTICAL APPLICATIONS

Important spiritual lessons can be learned from the larger aspects of Jesus' ministry that we have studied here. Consider the following facts to see what practical applications you can derive from them:

1. Most of the years of Jesus' life were *preparatory* to His public ministry.

2. Jesus was not popular for very long.

3. Jesus continued to minister, even under intense fire of hatred and jealousy.

4. The severest opposition could not cause Jesus' death prematurely. The hour of the cross was according to divine schedule.

5. Jesus' ministry was in life *and* in death.

6. Jesus came to give, not to take away.

The next nine lessons are devoted to a closer look at the various parts of Jesus' biography. As you study each part, refer to Chart J for setting recall. You would do well to memorize this chart.

Lesson 6
Preparation Period

We now begin more detailed study of aspects of Jesus' life but not just an academic analysis of a great man. There should be a spiritual fervor constraining us to learn more about the One who not only came to this world but also took up His habitation in our own hearts when He saved us. It has been correctly observed, "There is only one light by which you can read the life of Christ—the light of the life you now lead in the flesh; and that not the natural, but the won life.... 'Christ liveth in me.'"

Thus "with reverence, and a deep sense of its transcendent wonder,"[1] let the great subject of the life of Christ be approached.

It would be impossible for this short study guide to devote much space to any one event in Jesus' life. Instead, study suggestions are given to the reader so that he may (1) recognize the *highlights* of Jesus' life[2]; (2) discover the underlying purposes of Jesus; (3) see the *underlying purposes* of Jesus' ministry, involving such things as cause and effect, and progression to the ultimate goal of the cross; and (4) learn and apply the spiritual principles that the gospels so strongly and passionately teach.

The first thirty years of Jesus' life are years about which we know little. His birth, baptism, and wilderness temptation are three of the events in this period that are given special prominence by the gospels. About other things the record is sparse. This intended imbalance should be seen as a clue as to where we should direct our greatest attention.

1. G. Campbell Morgan, *The Crises of the Christ* (New York: Revell, 1936), p. 17.
2. One might reduce the number of high points in Jesus' career to the minimal number seven, represented by: birth, baptism, temptation, transfiguration, crucifixion, resurrection, and ascension. Morgan calls these "crises."

The gospels devote more space to events leading up to Jesus' birth than they do to the birth itself. This is also true of at least two oth- er crises in Jesus' career: the crucifixion and the resurrection. It is almost as if writers are compelled to spend many words in re- cording events surrounded by so much mystery and crucialness.

All the items leading up to the nativity account itself serve as preludes to the grand and simple theme of the birth of the Christ Child. Each prelude spotlights that theme from a different vantage point, and the reader of the gospels is made to eagerly anticipate the record of that eventful moment of God's entrance into the stream of humanity.

This great event in world history, Jesus' birth, took place without the world's realizing it at the time. But there were some individuals to whom this birth was announced beforehand. This is the subject of the preludes mentioned above. After you have read each "announcement" in the gospels, record some important facts concerning it in the spaces provided on Chart K. For example: (1) How is Jesus identified in each announcement? (2) What is the re- action of each person on hearing the announcement?

Now read the beautiful story of Jesus' birth (Luke 2:1-7). Ob- serve its simplicity and how matter of factly it is recorded. What is the significance attached to these parts of the story?
political: "decree from Caesar Augustus" (2:1)

_____

_____

economic: "should be taxed"; "no room . . . in the inn"

_____

geographic: "Bethlehem" ("house of bread"); (cf. Micah 5:2)

_____

_____

Try to derive more than one spiritual lesson from this passage. What is the real beauty of the nativity scene?

_____

_____

33

The Informed Ones		The Announcements of Jesus' Birth
"Home"	Elizabeth (Luke 1:39-45)	
	Zechariah (Luke 1:16-17)	
"Clergy" ("new" prophets who lived after Malachi).	Simeon (Luke 2:25-35)	
	Anna (Luke 2:36-38)	
"Laity"	Shepherds (Luke 2:8-20)	
"Intelligentsia"	Wise men (astrologers) (Gentiles) (Matt. 2:1-12)	
"Royalty" and "Citizenry"	Herod and people (Matt. 2:1-6)	
"Handmaid of the Lord" and	Mary (Luke 1:26-38, 46-56)	
"Descendant of a king"	Joseph (Matt. 1:18-25)	

II. FROM INFANCY TO MANHOOD

If you are working with a harmony of the gospels, you will observe that Matthew and Luke are the only writers who relate events of Jesus' life between His birth and public ministry. After you have read each of the passages below, answer the questions given and follow other study suggestions. Throughout your study of the narrative of Jesus' life always look for the main truths taught by each event, including what may be learned about Jesus Himself.

A. Circumcision and Naming (Luke 2:21: Matt. 1:25*b*)

What was the symbolical intention of the rite of circumcision?

_____

_____

(For your answer, read Gen. 17:1-14; Lev. 12:3.) What does the name "Jesus" mean? (Cf. Matt. 1:21. Note: As indicated earlier, the word Christ, a title of Jesus, from the Greek *chriō,* "anoint," means "the anointed one," or the Messiah.)

B. Dedication (Luke 2:22-38)

When Jesus was forty days old, He was presented to God in a service of dedication. Read Leviticus 12:1-8, which gives the law of purification of the mother, and Exodus 13:2-16, which asserts God's claim to the firstborn son in a Jewish home. How is holiness emphasized in these passages?

_____

_____

How does this apply to Jesus?

_____

What spiritual lesson may be learned from the reactions of Simeon and Anna when they realized who the Infant Jesus was?

_____

_____

C. Visit of The Wise Men (Matt. 2:1-12)

Write down some of your thoughts on the subjects suggested by these phrases:

"Where is he . . . ?" (2:2).

_____

"We have seen his star" (2:2).

_____

"We have . . . come to worship him" (2:2).

_____

_____

"They presented unto him gifts" (2:11).

_____

_____

D. Flight into Egypt (Matt. 2:13-18)

How do you reconcile the omnipotence of God and (1) the family's flight from danger; (2) the extensive carnage by a human ruler, Herod?

E. Home in Nazareth (Matt. 2:19-23: Luke 2:39*b*-40)

Jesus was often referred to as a Nazarene because Nazareth is where He was brought up by His parents. When His enemies called Him a Nazarene, their intent was one of scorn. Such scorn was prophesied by some of the prophets (cf. Isa. 53:3; Ps. 22:6; Dan. 9:26). The word *Nazareth* does not appear in the Old Testament, though the Hebrew word *netzar* ("shoot") of Isaiah 11:1 may have a connection with Matthew's reference in 2:23.

Read Luke 2:40 again, and observe which phrases refer to the physical, mental, and spiritual growth of Jesus, respectively. Does the fact of growth imply imperfection in the one growing?

F. Visit to the Temple (Luke 2:41-50)

This story clearly teaches that Jesus had a keen awareness of His divine mission at a young age. Just how many details of that mission He knew at age twelve is not revealed. But we must not be misled by what are the limitations of knowledge in a normal youth of twelve. Jesus was an extraordinary twelve-year-old. For evidence of this, compare His understanding with that of the people and teachers (2:47), and of His parents (2:50).

G. From Age Twelve to Thirty (Luke 2:51-52)

What do these verses reveal about the maturing years of Jesus' life?

---

3. Jesus was around thirty years old when He began His public ministry (Luke 3:23).

Try to project a background to these descriptions from other known or inferred facts, such as:

1. His parents were godly people. His father, Joseph, may have died when Jesus was a youth, for he is not referred to later in the gospels, whereas His mother, brothers, and sisters are.

2. He had brothers and sisters. Two brothers (James and Jude) wrote epistles of the Bible.

3. His education was received partly at home, partly in the village synagogue. Of this "poor man's education," James Stalker writes:

> As the scribes contemptuously said, He had never learned, or, as we should say, He was not college-bred. No; but the love of knowledge was early awake within Him. He daily knew the joy of deep and happy thought; He had the best of all keys to knowledge—the open mind and the loving heart; and the three great books lay ever open before Him—the Bible, Man, and Nature.[4]

4. Jesus knew three languages: Hebrew, Greek, and Aramaic. The last two were vernacular languages of His day; Hebrew was the language of Israel's Scriptures and religious services, and of secular literature.

5. He learned and engaged in the trade of His father: carpentry. If Jesus' father died prematurely, Jesus the firstborn was probably the family's main breadwinner.

6. Jesus must have spent much time outdoors, for He was a lover of nature. Refer to a map of Palestine, and note the location of Nazareth. All descriptions of the region around Nazareth agree on its natural beauty. Note also that Jesus did not live far from the Sea of Galilee, where He may have gone fishing in His young years.

H. Jesus' Baptism (Matt. 3:13-17; Mark 1:9-11; Luke 3:21-23a)

Jesus was about thirty years old when He bade His family and friends of Nazareth farewell and moved to the environs of Jerusalem. Before He would launch out on His public work, however, two preparatory experiences were to be His: baptism and temptations by Satan.

Note how many people had been thronging around John the Baptist to hear him preach, and to be baptized of him (Matt. 3:5-7; Mark 1:5, 7). Then Jesus came to John "to be baptized of him"

4. James Stalker, *The Life of Jesus Christ*, rev. ed. (Westwood, N.J.: Revell, 1891), pp. 20-21.

3:13). (See John 1:28 for the location of John's baptismal
es.) Why was Jesus baptized? In attempting to answer this
tion, consider the following:

1. John's reticence (Matt. 3:14)
2. Jesus' answer (Matt. 3:15)
3. Jesus had no sins to repent of, though John's preaching and
baptism concerned repentance (Matt. 3:11).
4. John's ministry as forerunner and herald of Jesus was now
coming to a close; and Jesus' public ministry was about to
commence.

Some see Jesus' baptism a symbolic identification of the Saviour with men, foretelling His substitutionary work. A more like-
ly explanation seems to be that here is a symbolic inaugural rite
signifying the end of the old dispensation and the initiation of the
new. The new was to replace the old, and the Person who was to
fulfill God's righteousness was now coming on the scene. Reflect
on the following formal introduction to the world: "This is my beloved Son, in whom I am well pleased" (Matt. 3:17).

I. Jesus Tempted in the Wilderness (Matt. 4:1-11; Mark 1:12-13;
Luke 4:1-13)

The gospels record three temptations that were hurled at Jesus by
Satan in the wilderness of Judah. (Matthew's order is perhaps the
chronological one.) There were other temptations during these
forty days, just as Jesus was tempted throughout His earthly life.
(Cf. Luke 4:13.) But never did He sin by *yielding* to any temptation.
Read the story, and then compare the three temptations, recording your observations on Chart L.
1. The temptations that Satan puts to a believer are always related
to the circumstances and experiences of the believer at that time.
How relevant was the first temptation to Jesus' physical experience?

_____

_____

Considering the material and political nature of the kingdom that
the Jews were seeking at this time, how relevant were all the
temptations to One who would now claim to be the Messiah?

_____

_____

38

Matthew's Order	The "Ifs"	The Actual Temptation	Realm of the Temptation	Jesus Answers by Scripture
1. Stones				(Deut. 8:3)
2. Pinnacle				(Ps. 91:11-12; Deut. 6:16)
3. Kingdoms				(Deut. 6:13)

2. What spiritual lessons for Christian living are to be learned from this account?

_____

_____

III. SUMMARY

The thirty preparation years of Christ's life anticipated the day and hour when the Son of God would come out into the arena of the populace and fulfill the ministry that His Father sent Him to do. Never was He behind the divine schedule, or ahead.

The gospels record more actions and words of the people than they do of Jesus in this preparation period. And yet, Jesus is the central character of the story. This is seen when we summarize the contents of the narrative thus:

1. announcements	ABOUT	Jesus
2. worship directed	TO	Jesus the Child
3. care	OF	Jesus the Lad
4. words spoken	TO	Jesus

For a review exercise, pursue this point further, noting that the few recorded words spoken by Jesus were really brought on by *questions* asked by teachers, His parents, and John, and by *challenges* hurled by Satan.

Lesson 7

Beginning of Public Ministry Period

The public ministry of Jesus lasted about three and one-half years, with the first as the year of obscurity. During this year Jesus emerged from virtual obscurity into public notice, gradually rising to a peak of popularity. The second year was spent wholly in Galilee, where His most extensive work was accomplished. Toward the end of this year His popularity waned and His enemies became more numerous and persistent. The third year, the Year of Opposition, was when He fulfilled those ministries that needed to be done before He was to die, such as training His disciples for the proclamation of the gospel.

> Thus the life of the Savior in its external outline resembles that of many a reformer and benefactor of mankind. Such a life often begins with a period during which the public is gradually made aware of the new man in its midst, then passes into a period when his doctrine or reform is borne aloft on the shoulders of popularity, and ends with a reaction, when the old prejudices and interests that have been assailed by him rally from his attack and, gaining to themselves the passions of the crowd, crush him in their rage.[1]

As we begin our study of the first part of Jesus' public ministry—Opening Events—it will help us to get a perspective of the whole. Chart M, adapted from Chart J, gives this perspective and also indicates what lessons of the study guide are devoted to the various parts of Jesus' ministry.

---

1. James Stalker, *The Life of Jesus Christ*, rev. ed. (Westwood, N.J.: Revell, 1891), p. 48.

I. FIRST INTRODUCTIONS (John 1:19-34)

It was John the Baptist who formally introduced Jesus to the multitudes as Jesus began His public ministry. Before that introduction is recorded by the gospel writer in John 1:29-34, the introducer himself, John the Baptist, is identified in 1:19-28. Read these verses carefully. Note the repeated question, "Who art thou?" Analyze John's various answers. What was John especially trying to get across to the people?

_____

_____

THE CREST OF MINISTRY   **Chart M**

PUBLIC MINISTRY					
FIRST YEAR		SECOND YEAR		THIRD YEAR	
Obscurity		Popularity		Opposition	
4 months OPENING EVENTS	8 months EARLY MINISTRIES	14 months EXTENDED MINISTRIES		6 months SPECIALIZED MINISTRY	6 months CONCLUDING MINISTRIES
		EARLY GALILEAN	MIDDLE GALILEAN		
Lesson 7	8	9	10	11	12

A. God Introduces Jesus to John (John 1:32-34)

When Jesus was baptized, God introduced Him to John as His beloved Son (Matt. 3:16-17). Later, when John was introducing Jesus to the multitudes, he testified of this earlier experience. (Read John 1:32-34.) Note that a supernatural sign attended this introduction. What was it?

_____

Was John convinced?

What is the significance of God's commendation of Jesus, "in whom I am well pleased," in view of the fact that Jesus as of this time had not even begun His public ministry?

B. John Introduces Jesus to the Multitudes (John 1:29-31; cf. vv. 35-36)

What a way to be introduced to the world! "Behold the Lamb of God, which taketh away the sin of the world!" Try to picture the scene: multitudes are standing around John, all eyes fixed on him as though he were their deliverer. Then John's eye caught the form of Jesus walking toward him, and he seized the crowd's attention with a mighty "Behold!" The baptizer called out, "The Lamb of God, which taketh away the sin of the world! This is the one!"

As you study this brief passage, tarry long over the significance of such an introduction. John might have introduced Jesus as King, for King He was, and the word King is what the Jews' ears were itching to hear. Why did he identify Him as the Lamb, the slain Lamb?

(Note: John did not have to say "slain"; the Jews who knew their Scriptures were well aware that only a sacrificed lamb was associated with the taking away of sins—cf. Lev. 4:32-35; Isa. 53:7-8.)

II. FIRST FOLLOWERS (John 1:35-51)

The main purposes of Jesus' public ministry were to teach and help and then to die vicariously for the sins of the world. Jesus knew that these ministries would avail only for those who would choose to follow Him. Hence His constant invitation to people to become His disciples (literally, "learners"), His followers. In this passage John has recorded an interesting story of how Jesus won His first disciples.

Study the passage carefully. Use Chart N to record your observations of key subjects in each paragraph.[2] Look in the passage for such things as:

1. titles ascribed to Jesus
2. *following* Jesus
3. appearances of "found," "see"
4. personal testimonies
5. what is revealed of Jesus here

JOHN 1:35-51   **Chart N**

35
40
43
47
51

When you have observed and recorded the items listed above, reconstruct the story around these key truths. For example, account for the new title Messiah, since earlier Jesus had been called Rabbi (teacher). Also, contrast the titles of Jesus in the third paragraph with those of the fourth. What are some important spiritual truths taught by this passage?

_____

_____

_____

2. If you have used the analytical chart method of study in other books of this study guide, you may choose to so analyze this passage. The analytical chart method is fully described by the author, Irving L. Jensen, *Independent Bible Study* (Chicago: Moody, 1963).

III. FIRST MIRACLE (John 2:1-12)

On the third day of Jesus' journey to Cana from the place where He had won His first disciples, Jesus attended a marriage feast (which in Jesus' time often lasted for several days). As you read this story, observe how various needs were met by Jesus. Record these in Chart O.

HOW NEEDS WERE MET BY JESUS   **Chart O**

Persons	Needs	How Needs Were Met
Host		(v. 9)
Mary		(vv. 4-5)
Guests		(v. 11)
Disciples		(v. 11)

Various aspects of Jesus are seen in this story. He is:

A. Creator

His role as Creator is seen in His confrontation with the elements and laws of nature. Miracles by the Son of God, as recorded in the gospels, are as natural a part of the record as are deeds of kindness shown by the Son of Man. Concerning miracles, Frederic W. Farrar has said, "The word Nature has little or no meaning unless it be made to include the idea of its Author."[3]

B. Sovereign Word

His role as the sovereign Word is seen in His identifying His work as independent of the creature, even one so dear to Him as His mother. It was necessary for Jesus to show Mary that "henceforth He was not Jesus the Son of Mary, but the Christ the Son of God . . . that His thoughts were not as her thoughts, neither His

---

3. Frederic W. Farrar, *The Life of Christ* (Hartford, Conn.: Scranton, 1876), p. 148. See Lesson 15 for a discussion of Jesus' miracles.

ways her ways. It could not have been done in a manner more decisive, yet at the same time more entirely tender.[4]

C. Giver of Whole Life

His role as the giver of whole life is seen in His sharing and preserving the joys of the wedding occasion.
What are your own personal reactions to this inspired account of Jesus' miracles?

_____

What is the difference between a faith that brings on a miracle and a faith that a miracle brings on?

_____

_____

IV. SUMMARY

Review the gospel narratives that you have studied in this lesson and write a list of identifications of Jesus as He was revealed to the public in the opening events of His public ministry. This is the Jesus who, accompanied by His mother, brothers, and disciples, left Cana after the wedding and journeyed to Capernaum, readying Himself for a more open ministry among the multitudes (John 2:12).

4. Ibid., p. 144.

Lesson 8
Early Judean Period

The annual passover, most important of the Jewish holidays, brought Jews to Jerusalem from all over the world. It was celebrated in the middle of the first month of the religious calendar, Nisan (our April). The first Passover to be held during Jesus' public career brought Him from Galilee to Jerusalem, where He launched His Early Judean ministry (John 2:13). During this period, which lasted about eight months, Jesus thrust Himself openly and vigorously upon the crowds who had come to Jerusalem to celebrate the very feast that anticipated His own death. Little did they realize that the Lamb was standing in their midst.

Most of what we know about Christ's Early Judean ministry is supplied only by John's gospel. From what John was inspired to include in His narrative, we learn that what Jesus engaged in during these months was the very ministries that were to occupy Him throughout His career. These ministries were:

1. signs—identification of authority
2. interviews—demonstration of love

Our study of this lesson is centered on these Judean ministries of Jesus, from the time He came to Jerusalem from Galilee (John 2:13) to the time He returned to Galilee (John 4:4).

I. SIGNS: IDENTIFICATION OF AUTHORITY

A. First Cleansing of the Temple (John 2:13-22)[1]

When Jesus viewed the desecration of the Temple by the merchandise traffickers in the Court of the Gentiles, He drove out the

---

1. There is a second similar cleansing at the close of Jesus' ministry, recorded in Mark 11:15-18 (cf. Matt. 21:12-13 and Luke 19:45-48).

merchants, severely rebuking them for defiling His Father's house. The onlookers stood by helpless, awed no doubt at His presence, and asked for credentials that authorized such violent action. Their question was basically, "Who are you?"

1. How did Jesus identify Himself in verse 16?

In verse 19?

How did His disciples identify Him in verse 17? (Read Ps. 69:9.)

---

2. Analyze Jesus' prophecy (v. 19). What is the subject of the verb "destroy"?

How was this prophecy misquoted by the mobs three years later when Jesus was hanging on the cross? (Matt. 27:40)

What is the significance of Jesus' prophecy of His death and resurrection being spoken so early in His ministry?

Does verse 22 imply whether or not the disciples recognized Jesus' prophecy when it was first spoken?

B. Miracles (John 2:23-25)

Jesus identified His authority and power in constructive ways as well, by performing miracles, most of which were of a healing nature. The emphasis of this paragraph is the response of the people. The text says, "Many believed in his name." What kind of belief was this, in view of the verses that follow? (2:24-25; cf. 3:2; 8:30-59; 12:42-43).

II. INTERVIEWS: DEMONSTRATION OF LOVE

Jesus was the master evangelist. He ministered to large audiences in mass evangelism, and He ministered to individual souls in personal evangelism. By the former He demonstrated His concern for *all* people; by the latter He showed His interest and love for *each* person. Stalker has written, "A man who preaches to thousands with enthusiasm may be a mere orator, but the man who seeks the opportunity of speaking closely of the welfare of their souls to individuals must have a real fire from heaven burning in his heart.[2]

About nineteen private interviews by Jesus are cited in the gospels. Two of His longest recorded interviews are those that took place in His Early Judean ministry. One was with a man; the other with a woman. The man is identified by name; the woman is identified only by city. The man was a religious ruler of the Jewish Sanhedrin. The woman was an immoral wife. The man sought Jesus in secret; Jesus initiated the interview with the woman in broad daylight. As you study these two interviews you will want to look for further comparisons.

A. Interview with Nicodemus (John 3:1-21)[3]

1. What are Nicodemus's questions and Jesus' answers?

Note that Jesus' answer of verse 3 is to a question not stated in verse 2. What basically was the question of Nicodemus's heart?

---

2. Jesus identifies salvation with seeing "the kingdom of God" (vv. 3, 5). What verses tell of God's part in salvation?

Where is the first reference to *man's* part?

---

2. James Stalker, *The Life of Jesus Christ,* rev. ed. (Westwood, N.J.: Revell, 1891), p. 79.
3. The interview may have ended with v. 15, with John expanding the theme in vv. 16-21. If this be so, vv. 16-21 may still be taken as the essence of the evangel that Jesus Himself preached. Note the similarity of vv. 15 and 16.

How is this developed in the verses that follows?

_____

_____

B. Interview with the Woman of Sychar (John 4:5-30)

Jesus wasted no time in getting the woman's attention focused on her real need: salvation. After you have read the interview a few times, write down the things that were said about:
Salvation:

_____

_____

Way of salvation:

_____

_____

The Saviour:

_____

_____

Develop this study further, noting such things as: why Jesus said the things He said; the place of true worship in one's life; Jesus' self-consciousness of His deity. Throughout the gospels it is made clear that Jesus could do what He did (works) only because of who He was (Person). Observe in this interview that Jesus began with talking about who He was. Read 4:10.

You may also want to study this interview for what it teaches about methods of personal evangelism. This is a classic passage on this subject.

III. PREACHING AND TEACHING: EXPOSITION OF TRUTH

A. In Judea (John 3:22-4:3)

Before Jesus left Judea for His extensive Galilean ministry, He had opportunity to preach and teach to multitudes in the country regions. Many believed Jesus' message and were baptized by His disciples (cf. John 3:26; 4:1-2).

The success of Jesus' preaching mission was the occasion for John the Baptist, who was still going about urging the people to prepare their hearts to receive the Messiah, to again publicly magnify this Man Jesus as the promised Messiah, the Son of God. Analyze John's testimony of Christ in John 3:27-36, observing the many ways he identified Jesus. In the very heart of his testimony he exclaimed, "He must increase, but I must decrease" (3:30). What a wonderful life purpose for any believer!

B. In Samaria (John 4:4-42)[4]

The success of Jesus' preaching in Judea was also the occasion for Him to leave those parts and head for Galilee. For trouble was brewing in Judea, stirred by the Pharisees (John 4:1). Furthermore, Herod the tetrarch had just imprisoned John the Baptist (Luke 3:19-20; Mark 1:14; Matt. 4:12). This was the signal for Jesus to move, for He had a work to do in Galilee before He would give Himself over to the enemy to be killed.

The most direct route to Galilee was through Samaria and, although Jews avoided going through this "defiled" land,[5] Jesus traveled here, for Samaritans were part of His parish.

We have already studied Jesus' interview with the woman of Sychar. So impressed was the woman with meeting Christ that she hastened into the city and spread the word around concerning Him. Many believed as a result of her testimony, and "many more believed" after they listened to Jesus preaching and teaching for two days in their midst.

1. Read again verse 42. Recall what Jesus had said about salvation in 4:22b. How significant was it that *Samaritans* were recognizing Jesus as "Saviour of the *world*" (4:42)?

_____

IV. SUMMARY

1. How important was it for the people to know accurately who Jesus was?

_____

_____

4. Jesus' brief ministry in Samaria is arbitrarily considered part of His early Judean ministry since His Galilean tour began when he reached Galilee.
5. The Samaritans were half Jews. The hostility between the two nations was traceable back to the time when Jews returned from the Babylonian captivity to Canaan, where the Samaritans were already living.

2. What were Jesus' various methods in revealing His identity in this Early Judean period of His ministry?

_____

_____

_____

_____

3. List the names and titles by which He was recognized in the passages you have read for this lesson.

_____

_____

_____

_____

Lesson 9
Early Galilean Period

Seven hundred years before Christ, Isaiah foretold that the gospel would one day shine over Galilee. Read Isaiah 9:1-2 and Matthew 4:14-16. That day had now arrived, as Jesus crossed the border into Galilee. For thirty years He had lived here as Son of a carpenter; now He came to declare Himself Christ, the Son of God.

When Jesus left Judea and Samaria to go into Galilee, He was not unprepared for the opposition that would eventually come to Him there, for He was well aware that "a prophet hath no honour in his own country" (John 4:44; cf. Luke 4:24; Mark 6:4; Matt. 13:57). At least He could count on temporary favor and popularity, for devout Galileans who had recently attended the Passover in Jerusalem had seen Him do some wonderful things there, and these would serve as a warm reception committee on His arrival in Galilee. Jesus wanted to accomplish His mission in Galilee while the door was still open, knowing that soon that door would close by the hands of jealous religious leaders and the multitudes held captive in their sway.

Jesus spent about twenty months of His total public ministry in Galilee. About fourteen months of this time are called the Extended Ministries Period, because this is when most of His public work was accomplished. This period is also called the Year of Popularity, for He reached a peak of favor during this time, though the popularity gradually diminished, giving way to open opposition, which continued to the end of His life.

Review Chart J for orientation in your studies of this lesson. Chart P is an excerpt from Chart J. The Early Galilean Period is the subject of this lesson.

Since all of Jesus' extended ministries took place in the regions of Galilee, you should study carefully the geography of this land. Refer to a map, and note such things as:

52

FIRST YEAR		SECOND YEAR		THIRD YEAR		
Obscurity		Popularity		Opposition		
opening events	early ministries	extended ministries		specialized ministry	concluding ministries	
—	EARLY JUDEAN	EARLY GALILEAN	MIDDLE GALILEAN	LATER GALILEAN	LATER JUDEAN	PEREAN

1. *General location*. Galilee was the northernmost section of the Jewish homeland. Note that it borders on the Sea of Galilee.

2. *Size*. Galilee was about sixty miles by thirty miles, having a population estimated by some to be more than three million.

3. *Main cities*. There were more than two hundred cities and villages in Galilee. Those where Jesus spent most of His time were Nazareth, Cana, Capernaum, Magdala, Chorazin, and Nain. Capernaum was the center of His Galilean campaigns. If four cities of Christ's life were cited as key cities, they would be:

Bethlehem: city of birth
Nazareth: city of upbringing
Capernaum: center of evangelistic campaigns
Jerusalem: His city by right; place of His death

4. *Terrain*. Most of Galilee is an elevated plateau with irregular mountain masses. Most of Jesus' ministries were along the western shores of the Sea of Galilee. Study a topographical map, and visualize a typical journey of more than twenty-five miles from Nazareth to Capernaum.

Note: Because of the large amount of biblical text in this lesson and the ones to follow, it is recommended that the lesson be studied in various units. Take on no more material for one unit than what you can study carefully.

Chart Q shows the various parts of the Early Galilean Period.[1] Become acquainted with it, and refer to it often as you proceed in your study. Fill in the column titled Type of Ministry. You will find

1. The harmonies of Albert Cassel Wieand, *The Life of Our Lord* (Chicago: Moody, 1958) and A.T. Robertson, *A Harmony of the Gospels for Students of the Life of Christ* (New York: Harper, 1922) are generally followed in this study guide for the chronology of Jesus' life.

it helpful to use a harmony of the gospels for easier reference to the different gospels recording the same event.

For each of the stages shown on the chart, follow these general procedures of study:

1. Before making any comparative study of the gospels for any one event, read the full account of the stage as it is recorded in one gospel, then read it in another gospel, and so on. The purpose of this is to observe the *continuity* of Jesus' steps. For example, for Stage II, read Mark 1:14*b*-34 first; then read the passages listed under Luke and Matthew.

2. Underline key words and phrases in the Bible as you read.

3. Record such general things as the main emphasis of the mission of Jesus.

4. Continue your study by following the suggestions given below.

5. Conclude your study by listing spiritual applications of the truths recorded in the story.

Note: Follow the above procedures also for similar lessons to come.

I. STAGE I: THROUGHOUT GALILEE

A. General Description

1. How large was the extent of Jesus' early Galilean ministry? (Luke 4:14*b*-15)

_____

B. Nobleman's Son Healed (John 4:46-54)

1. What kind of belief is Jesus describing in verse 48?

_____

2. Note the contrasting words "come" and "go" in verses 49 and 50. What is taught here concerning Jesus' *method* of miracle working?

_____

_____

3. What kind of belief was the nobleman's at the point of verse 50?

_____

STAGES and EVENTS	TYPE OF MINISTRY	MATTHEW	MARK	LUKE	JOHN
Return to Galilee		4:12	1:14a	4:14a	4:43-45
STAGE I: THROUGHOUT GALILEE GENERAL DESCRIPTION: Teaching Nobleman's Son Healed (Cana) First Rejection at Nazareth (Nazareth)				4:14b-15 4:16-30	4:46-54

STAGE II: AT CAPERNAUM
GENERAL DESCRIPTION:
  Preaching, Teaching
  Call of Four Fishermen
  A Day of Miracles
  1. Demoniac Healed
    (forenoon)
  2. Peter's Mother-in-law
    Healed (afternoon)
  3. Many Healed (evening)
		4:13-17
		
		4:18-22
		
		8:14-15
		8:16-17
			1:14b-15
			
			1:16-20
			
			1:21-28
			
			1:29-31
			1:32-34
				4:31-32
				
				5:1-11
				
				4:33-37
				
				4:38-39
				4:40-41	

STAGE III: THROUGHOUT GALILEE
GENERAL DESCRIPTION:
  Preaching and Healing
  Leper Healed
		4:23-24
		8:2-4
			1:35-39
			1:40-45
				4:42a-44
				5:12-16	

STAGE IV: AT CAPERNAUM
GENERAL DESCRIPTION:
  Preaching, Teaching, Healing
  Paralytic Forgiven and Healed
  Call of Matthew
  Three Parables
		9:2-8
		9:9-13
		9:14-17
			2:1-2
			2:3-12
			2:13-17
			2:18-22
				5:17
				5:18-26
				5:27a-32
				5:33-39	

Describe his belief at verse 53.

_____

_____

C. First Rejection At Nazareth (Luke 4:16-30)

1. How does the quote from Isaiah (61:1-2) describe the ministry of Jesus?

_____

What were the people's desperate needs?

_____

2. At one point the people received Jesus' words as "gracious words" (4:22). Later, His words infuriated them. What brought on the change?

_____

3. What tremendous miracle do you see in verse 30?

_____

_____

II. STAGE II: AT CAPERNAUM

A. General Description (Matt. 4:13-17; Mark 1:14b-15; Luke 4:31-32)

Read Isaiah 9:1-7 for background to Matthew's Old Testament quote. What was the people's spiritual condition?

_____

1. What was the basic message of Jesus' preaching and teaching, according to Matthew and Mark?

_____

_____

2. Note the references to time, event, message, and commands in Mark 1:15.
3. What does the word "gospel" mean? (Consult a Bible dictionary if necessary.)

_____

4. Account for Matthew's "kingdom of heaven" (Matt. 4:17) and Mark's "kingdom of God" (Mark 1:15). For help in answering this, recall your comparative study of the four gospels in Lesson 2. Also, you may want to refer to a Bible dictionary or commentary for a comparative study of these phrases.

_____

_____

B. Call of Four Fishermen (Matt. 4:18-22; Mark 1:16-20; Luke 5:1-11)

1. Which gospel gives the most details?

_____

2. Note the contrast in Luke of *failure* in fishing (5:5) and *success* in fishing (5:9-10). What spiritual lessons about personal soul-winning are taught here?

_____

_____

3. Why did Jesus use the phrase "fishers of men"?

_____

_____

In speaking to James and John might He have talked of "menders of men"?

_____

4. Recall that Andrew and Peter were among those who followed Jesus at an earlier time (John 1:35-51). The formation of the apostolate (twelve apostles) could be said to be in three stages: (1) initial commitment to follow; (2) constant company, learning and helping (this is the call of the present passage); and (3) apostolic service, continuing Christ's ministry to the multitudes.

C. A Day of Miracles

1. Demoniac healed (Mark 1:21-28; Luke 4:33-37). In what two ways did Jesus demonstrate His authority?

_____

How important is it today for the Christian witness to have a ring of authority?

_____

_____

2. Peter's mother-in-law healed (Matt. 8:14-15; Mark 1:29-31; Luke 4:38-39). Note that all three gospels report that Peter's mother-in-law served Jesus and others in the house after she was healed. Significance?

_____

_____

3. Many healed (Matt. 8:16-17; Mark 1:32-34; Luke 4:40-41). Read Isaiah 53:4, which Matthew quotes. What is the *greater* fulfillment of this prophecy in Christ? See 1 Peter 2:24.

Why did Christ not allow the demons to testify concerning Him (Luke 4:41)?

Are the credentials of the messenger of no major importance as long as the message is true? Apply this to the Christian witness of the gospel.

III. STAGE III: THROUGHOUT GALILEE

A. General Description (Matt. 4:23-24; Mark 1:35-39; Luke 4:42a-44)

1. What different things does Mark 1:35 teach about Jesus' prayer life?

---

2. Observe the universal purpose and program of Jesus' ministry. Note that even Syrian Gentiles were attracted to Him (Matt. 4:24).

B. Leper Healed (Matt. 8:2-4; Mark 1:40-45; Luke 5:12-16)

1. Observe that Jesus' will, ability, and love were involved in this healing (Mark 1:40-41). Is it always Jesus' will to heal a sick person? If not, why not?

---

2. Why would the man's testimony of healing have been strengthened if the priest had first had the opportunity to declare the leprosy gone (according to Mosaic law, Lev. 13-14)?

_____

_____

3. Comment on Luke 5:16: "And he withdrew himself into the wilderness, and prayed."

_____

_____

IV. STAGE IV: AT CAPERNAUM

A. General Description (Mark 2:1-2; Luke 5:17)

1. How do these verses bear out the truth that Jesus was more concerned about preaching and teaching than healing? (Cf. Matt. 9:2).

_____

_____

B. Paralytic Forgiven and Healed (Matt. 9:2-8; Mark 2:3-12; Luke 5:18-26)

1. What was Jesus' first concern for the man?

_____

2. How much of the scribes' words of Mark 2:7 was true?

_____

3. How was the extent of Jesus' authority enlarged with this event?

_____

4. Did the people recognize Jesus as God after they saw this miracle? (Note Matt. 9:8.)

_____

C. Call of Matthew (Matt. 9:9-13; Mark 2:13-17; Luke 5:27a-32)

Publicans were tax collectors for the Roman state, despised by the people as greedy oppressors using illegal tools in their profession.

1. What is taught here about discipleship?

_____

Audience of the gospel?

_____

Fellowship of Christians?

_____

2. What did Jesus mean by quoting Hosea 6:6 (Matt. 9:13)?

_____

_____

3. Jesus said, "I am not come to call the righteous . . . " (Matt. 9:13). Whom did He have in mind, and in what sense did He call them "righteous"?

_____

_____

_____

D. Three Parables (Matt. 9:14-17; Mark 2:18-22; Luke 5:33-39)

The Pharisees kept a fast every Monday and Thursday (cf. Luke 18:12), and it is possible that Matthew's feast was on one of these days. Hence the challenging question directed to Jesus concerning His disciples. What was the one main point taught by Jesus in the three parables?

_____

What was the difference between the ministries of John the Baptist and Jesus? In this connection, compare the Old and New Testaments.

_____

_____

V. SUMMARY

As a summary exercise, compare the four general descriptions cited above as to what were Jesus' main purposes and activities in

this four-month Early Galilean Period. List important lessons you
have learned in your study of this lesson.

_____

_____

_____

_____

_____

_____

_____

_____

_____

Lesson 10
Middle Galilean Period

Jesus' extended ministry in Galilee was temporarily suspended after about four months for a visit to Jerusalem. The occasion was the annual Passover feast (John 5:1). When He returned subsequently to His hometown, Capernaum, He was ready to begin the most active and fruitful period of His public ministry. This is the Middle Galilean Period, which lasted about ten months.

Because of the large amount of text involved in the period being studied in this lesson, only the highlights can be emphasized. The outline in Chart R should be used as a reference for any further studies you may want to make in the stories of the gospels. Use the outline as an aid to keep from losing sight of the "forest" as you look at the "trees." If you do not choose to make an exhaustive comparative study of all the gospels for this lesson, it is recommended that you select one gospel and follow the narrative in it, referring to another gospel whenever the selected one does not record the event. All references are furnished in the outline.

Observe the following in the outline on pages 64 and 65:
1. The ministry in Galilee did not actually begin until Jesus returned from Jerusalem. Beginning with the second phase (NEAR THE SEA) note the alternating pattern of Jesus' ministry:

> NEAR THE SEA
> THROUGHOUT GALILEE
> BY THE SEA
> THROUGHOUT GALILEE
> BY THE SEA

Note that there was a return to Capernaum toward the end of each phase of this Middle Galilean Period.
2. As you read each story of each phase, record in the column headed MINISTRY the type of Jesus' ministry, of these: teaching, preaching, miracles (most of these were healing), training of dis-

ciples. After you have completed this study, note that on the tours THROUGHOUT GALILEE there was an emphasis on the Word ministry (teaching and preaching), while in the two phases BY THE SEA (IV and VI) there was an emphasis on works ministry (healing and other miracles). Recall from your previous studies what Christ's main purpose was in performing miracles.

3. Jesus was always trying to get the people to recognize *who* He was. Under the column REACTIONS record how He was recognized and received by the people and the disciples.

4. Note the Jerusalem opposition at the beginning of this period and the defection of some disciples at the end. Where in the course of the Middle Galilean Period was there another expression of opposition?

_____

_____

5. Note that John's gospel does not record much of this Middle Galilean Period.

It is difficult to determine any one outstanding pattern of Jesus' strategy during this period. He had in mind a ministry to His disciples as well as a ministry to people in all the towns and villages of Galilee. Capernaum was His headquarters, and a tour to any part of Galilee always began and ended at that city. Note this geographical pattern in the outline of this lesson.

I. TO JERUSALEM AND RETURN

Jesus used the occasion of this national holiday to reveal to the Jews more about *who* He was. Three controversies arose over the law concerning the Sabbath day.

A. Impotent Man Healed (John 5:1-47)

1. Observe the repeated word "Father." In what ways did Jesus show that He was the Son of God?

_____

_____

B. Plucking Grain (Matt. 12:1-8; Mark 2:23-28; Luke 6:1-5)

1. Now the enemies of Jesus hopefully shifted their accusations to His disciples. Observe how Jesus, in defending the disciples, rested the issue on who He was. How did He identify Himself here?

	Events	Location	Matthew	Mark	Luke	John	Ministry	Reactions
	I. TO JERUSALEM AND RETURN							
	1. Impotent man healed	John 5:1, Jerusalem				5:1-47		
	2. Plucking grain	—grainfields	12:1-8	2:23-28	6:1-5			
	3. Withered hand healed	—synagogue	12:9-14	3:1-6	6:6-11			ENEMIES PLOT HOW TO DESTROY HIM
	II. NEAR THE SEA (Galilee)	GALILEE						
	1. Thronging crowds	Mark 3:7, by the sea	12:15-21	3:7-12				
	2. Apostles ordained	Mark 3:13, hills	10:2-4	3:13-19	6:12-16			
	3. Sermon on the Mount	Luke 6:17, level place	5-7		6:17-49			
	4. RETURN to Capernaum; centurion's servant healed	Matt. 8:5, Capernaum	8:1, 5-13		7:1-10			
EMPHASIS ON WORD MINISTRY	**III. THROUGHOUT GALILEE**							
	1. Widow's son restored	Luke 7:11, Nain			7:11-17			
	2. John inquires of Jesus		11:2-19		7:18-35			
	3. Anointed by a woman				7:36-50			
	4. Preaching tour; RETURN to Capernaum	Luke 8:1, cities and villages		2:1	8:1-3			
	5. Opposition in Capernaum —relatives apprehensive	Mark 3:21, Capernaum	12:22-50	3:20-21, 31-35	8:19-21			
	—Scribes and Pharisees angry		12:22-45	3:22-30				
EMPHASIS ON WORKS MINISTRY	**IV. BY THE SEA**							
	1. Parables	Mark 4:1, beside sea	13:1-53	4:1-34	8:4-18			
	2. Tempest stilled	Mark 4:35, other side	8:18, 23-27	4:35-41	8:22-25			
	3. Demoniacs cured	Matt. 8:28	8:28-34	5:1-20	8:26-39			
	4. RETURN to Capernaum	Mark 5:1-20	9:1	5:21	8:40			
	5. Healings in Capernaum	Matt. 9:1	9:18-34	5:22-43	8:41-56			

MIDDLE GALILEAN PERIOD (continued)

Events	Location	Matthew	Mark	Luke	John	Ministry	Reactions
V. THROUGHOUT GALILEE *(EMPHASIS ON WORD MINISTRY)*							
1. Last visit to Nazareth	Matt. 13:54	13:54-58	6:1-6a				
2. Tour through Galilee	Matt. 9:35	9:35-38	6:6b				
3. Twelve sent out	Luke 9:6	10:1-42	6:7-13	9:1-6			
4. Jesus tours Galilee	Matt. 11:1	11:1					
5. King Herod disturbed		14:1-12	6:14-29	9:7-9			
6. Apostles RETURN to Capernaum	John 6:1		6:30	9:10			
VI. BY THE SEA *(EMPHASIS ON WORKS MINISTRY)*							
1. Brief visit with apostles	Luke 9:10b John 6:3	14:13					
2. Five thousand fed		14:14-21	6:31-33	9:10b-11a	6:1-3		
3. Solitary prayer	Mark 6:46	14:22-23a	6:34-44	9:11b-17	6:4-14		
4. Walking on water	John 6:17	14:23b-33	6:45-46		6:15		
5. Healing at Gennesaret	Matt. 14:34	14:34-36	6:47-52		6:16-21		
6. RETURN to Capernaum; teaching in synagogue	John 6:24, 59		6:53-56		6:22-59		
7. Forsaken by many disciples					6:60-71		MANY DISCIPLES FORSAKE HIM

C. Withered Hand Healed (Matt. 12:9-14; Mark 3:1-6; Luke 6:6-11)

1. Of what did Jesus show Himself to be Lord on this occasion?

___

That the Pharisees and Herodians, usually arch foes, got together to plot Jesus' murder, indicates the fury of their hearts.

II. NEAR THE SEA (GALILEE)

A. Thronging Crowds (Matt. 12:15-21; Mark 3:7-12)

1. What does Isaiah 42:1-4, quoted by Matthew, disclose regarding Jesus' avoiding public acclaim as such?

___

___

B. Apostles Ordained (Mark 3:13-19: Luke 6:12-16)

1. Note the duration of Jesus' prayer session (Luke 6:12). What should determine duration of prayer?

_____

_____

2. Observe that Jesus chose twelve from a larger group. Do we ever read of complaint by the others that they were not chosen?

_____

C. Sermon on the Mount (Matt. 5-7; Luke 6:17-49)

The location of the mountain with a level place is unknown. It was probably near Capernaum.

The kingdom message was not delivered to unbelievers to tell them how to enter the kingdom; rather, it was given primarily for the disciples' benefit to reveal truths about those who are citizens of the kingdom. Study carefully Matthew's account, and organize your observations around the following outline: Citizens of the Kingdom: (1) Character (5:1-16); (2) Requirements (5:17-48); (3) Motives (6:1-18); Conduct (6:19–7:12); Testing (7:13-27).
1. List ten important spiritual lessons taught by these chapters.

_____

_____

_____

_____

_____

_____

_____

_____

_____

_____

D. Return to Capernaum: Centurion's Servant Healed (Matt. 8:1; 5-13; Luke 7:1-10)

1. What does Jesus say here about Gentile believers and Jewish unbelievers?

_____

_____

The phrase "children of the kingdom" (Matt. 8:12) refers to Jews without true faith. Compare Romans 9:6-9.

III. THROUGHOUT GALILEE

A. Widow's Son Restored to Life (Luke 7:11-17)

1. Try to visualize the action of this extraordinary miracle. Is it difficult to imagine the fear that seized the people? What might people's reaction be today if they saw a similar miracle?

_____

_____

2. Why did Jesus limit this type of miracle to only a few occasions?

_____

B. John Inquires of Jesus (Matt. 11:2-19; Luke 7:18-35)

1. What good things did Jesus say about John (Matt.11:7-11)?

_____

_____

2. In light of this, was Jesus' reply to John's original question a severe rebuke (Matt. 11:2-6)?

_____

Probably John was expecting Jesus to execute judgment for sin at that time, whereas Jesus' ministry then was just the opposite. Hence John's honest but erring question. In His later words (Matt. 11:16-19) Jesus hinted at judgment to come.

C. Anointed by a Woman (Luke 7:36-50)

1. This story teaches some basic truths about salvation. Identify these:

> The ones needing salvation (7:39)
> One aspect of salvation (7:50)
> Requirements for salvation (7:47, 50)
> Fruit of salvation (7:50)

2. In view of the context, what was the cause of the woman's tears (7:38)?

_____

_____

D. Preaching Tour: Return to Capernaum (Luke 8:1-3; Mark 3:19*b*)

1. What main message did Jesus preach at this time?

_____

2. What do these verses disclose about the provision of Jesus' material needs?

_____

_____

3. Does the phrase "and the twelve were with him" suggest that at other times in Jesus' evangelistic tours the apostles were not with Him?

_____

_____

4. If so, what may they have been doing then?

_____

_____

E. Opposition in Capernaum (Matt. 12:22-50; Mark 3:20-35; Luke 8:19-21)

The words translated "his friends" (Mark 3:21) refer to Jesus' relatives. Their concern, "He is beside himself," does not refer to insanity but to overworked zeal. They were well intentioned in their concern, but wrong. Observe from Matthew 12:46-50 that Jesus would not let interference by His relatives hinder His ministry.

Note that the opposition by the scribes and Pharisees is traced back to Jerusalem (Mark 3:22). Study Jesus' reply to their charge that He did these miracles by Satanic power.

1. What lessons also are taught here about spoken words?

_____

_____

IV. BY THE SEA

A. Parables (Matt. 13:1-53; Mark 4:1-34; Luke 8:4-18)

More is said in Lesson 15 about Jesus' use of parables. Refer to this briefly. For your present study, identify the *main* truth taught by each parable, and record this in Chart S.

MAIN TRUTHS OF PARABLES   **Chart S**

Parable	Main Truth
Sower	
Candle and bushel	
Growing seed	
Tares	
Mustard seed	
Leaven	
Hidden treasure	
Pearl of great price	
Fishnet	
Householder	

Do not leave this important section without making personal applications from these very pertinent parables of Jesus.

69

B. Tempest Stilled (Matt. 8:23-27; Mark 4:35-41; Luke 8:22-25)

1. We might call this a parable in action. What weakness in the disciples is revealed here?

2. Did the disciples include Jesus when they said, "We perish" (Luke 8:24)?

Observe that here was a double miracle involving both wind and sea. If only the wind had been stilled, the waves would have continued for some time. Note the typical question about Jesus' identity: "Who then is this . . . ?" (Mark 4:41, ASV*).

C. Demonics Cured (Matt. 8:28-34; Mark 5:1-20; Luke 8:26-39)

1. New Testament demon possession and its symptoms, effects, and cure are extensively described in this narrative. What is taught here about the tremendous power of the satanic world?

2. How is Christ's greater power demonstrated?

3. Contrast the loss of a large and valuable herd of swine and the restoration of a man's mental health. Does Jesus have the authority to dispose of a man's wealth?

D. Return to Capernaum (Matt. 9:1; Mark 5:21; Luke 8:40)

Note how the city of Capernaum is identified in Matthew 9:1. Observe the welcome extended Jesus by the large crowd.

American Standard Bible.

E. Healings in Capernaum (Matt.9:18-34; Mark 5:22-43; Luke 8:41-56)

1. Four different instances of healing are recorded here. What is the common requisite for healing in the first three instances?

_____

2. Could the dumb demoniac express faith?

_____

3. Whose faith was honored in his case?

_____

Remember to record reaction on the outline chart given at the beginning of this lesson.

V. THROUGHOUT GALILEE

Time was running out for Jesus in regard to opportunities for itinerant evangelization in the many cities and villages of Galilee. There would still be opportunities for specialized ministries in Galilee, but now Jesus chose to make a last general tour of the land. The first stop on the tour was His hometown, Nazareth.

A. Last Visit to Nazareth (Matt. 13:54-58; Mark 6:1-6a)

1. What sad note is sounded by the phrase "and when he was come into his own country" (Matt. 13:54) in view of the context?

_____

_____

2. What is the tone of the words "this man" in the same verse?

_____

_____

3. Comment on Jesus' reaction of Mark 6:6a.

_____

_____

B. Tour Through Galilee (Matt.9:35-38; Mark 6:6b)

1. Observe how much information is compacted in the four verses of Matthew, such as: (1) extent of the tour, (2) ministries of Jesus,

(3) condition of the people, (4) reaction, evaluation, and recommendation of Jesus. Try to visualize harassed, helpless sheep without a shepherd. How does this describe unsaved people today?

_____

2. What may be learned from these verses about compassion and prayer?

_____

_____

_____

_____

C. Twelve Sent Out (Matt. 10:1-42; Mark 6:7-13; Luke 9:1-6)

Many practical lessons on Christian service are taught here. Study especially the Matthew passage. Observe the various things Jesus gave these twelve apostles, including authority, commission, instructions, warning, encouragement, and motivation.
1. What should be the supreme motive in all Christian service?

_____

D. Jesus Tours Galilee (Matt. 11:1)

1. After Jesus had sent out the six pairs of apostles (Mark 6:12-13; Luke 9:6), He went on His own evangelistic tour. What may have been His strategy in planning separate tours?

_____

Note that Jesus went to the cities (Matt. 11:1), whereas the apostles went to the towns (Luke 9:6; cf. also that only *towns* were referred to in Jesus' instructions given to the apostles above).

E. King Herod Disturbed (Matt. 14:1-12; Mark 6:14-29; Luke 9:7-9)

The main point of this story is not the parenthetical recounting of John the Baptist's death that had occurred earlier but the reaction of King Herod, ruler of Galilee and Perea, over the works of Jesus. Study this section with the outline in Chart T in mind.

We can understand the storm in Herod's heart when the memory of John the Baptist was revived, for he had murdered a

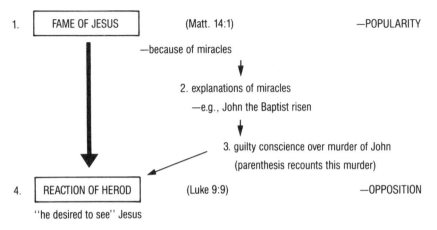

1.   FAME OF JESUS   (Matt. 14:1)   —POPULARITY

—because of miracles

2. explanations of miracles
—e.g., John the Baptist risen

3. guilty conscience over murder of John
(parenthesis recounts this murder)

4.   REACTION OF HEROD   (Luke 9:9)   —OPPOSITION

"he desired to see" Jesus

man whom he had recognized to be righteous and holy (Mark 6:20). Now Herod "kept seeking to see" Jesus (Luke 9:9*b*, literal trans.). He apparently had only evil intentions, for we observe that Jesus from this point on carefully avoided him. (Cf. Luke 13:31-32.) The crest of Jesus' popularity was now behind Him; the months ahead would bring increasing opposition.

F. Apostles Return to Capernaum (Mark 6:30; Luke 9:10)

The Passover holiday was near (John 6:4) when the twelve apostles returned to Capernaum after a couple of weeks of evangelizing, eager to report to Jesus of their ministries. Thus ended the last organized ministry throughout Galilee. Jesus still had some work to do in Galilee (cf. John 7:1), but this would not be extensive evangelization.

VI. BY THE SEA

A. Brief Visit with the Apostles (Matt.14:13; Mark 6:31-33; Luke 9:10*b*-11*b*; John 6:1-3)

1. What was Jesus' main purpose in leading the apostles to this retreat?

_____

_____

2. Does this suggest any spiritual truth?

_____

B. Five Thousand Fed (Matt. 14:14-21; Mark 6:34-44; Luke 9:11*b*-17; John 6:4-14)

1. What were the different needs of the people, and how were these filled by Jesus?

_____

_____

_____

2. What should the disciples have learned from this miracle?

_____

_____

After you answer the above question, read Mark 6:52.

C. Solitary Prayer (Matt. 14:22-23*a*; Mark 6:45-46; John 6:15)

1. What is the special value of solitary prayer?

_____

_____

2. What was probably the main burden of Jesus' heart at this time in view of the events that had recently transpired?

_____

_____

D. Walking on Water (Matt. 14:23*b*-33; Mark 6:47-52; John 6:16-21)

1. What miracles are recorded here?

_____

_____

2. Did Jesus give help despite the disciples' doubt?

_____

_____

3. How is this situation different from earlier ones, as at Nazareth when Jesus restricted His miracles because of unbelief?

_____

_____

E. Healing at Gennesaret (Matt. 14:33-36; Mark 6:53-56)

1. Note the method of healing here (Matt. 14:36). Was Jesus bound by method?

_____

_____

2. In your own words, what is a miracle?

_____

_____

F. Return to Capernaum; Teaching in Synagogue (John 6:22-59)

1. Here is recorded Christ's great discourse on the bread of life. What are the main words of this discourse?

_____

_____

2. Recall the joyous reaction of the five thousand over Jesus' recent multiplying of the physical bread, to appreciate the impact of this message about spiritual bread (cf. John 6:26-27). Is Christ a bread king?

_____

3. What place does He assign to the physical needs of mankind?

_____

_____

4. List the many tremendous statements made about eternal life. What did Jesus say about His Father's will?

_____

_____

_____

G. Forsaken by Many Disciples (John 6:60-71)

1. What is recorded here about:
(a) Many disciples:

_____

(b) Eleven of the twelve:

_____

(c) One of the twelve:

_____

VII. SUMMARY

Your study of this Middle Galilean Period has shown how much Jesus and the twelve accomplished in ten months. At the end of this period Passover time arrived (John 6:4). But Jesus did not go to Jerusalem to observe the feast because the Jews there were seeking to kill Him (John 7: 1). Jesus' time had not yet arrived (John 7:6). There was still a year of work to do before the sacrifice. Our next lesson looks at the first six months of that final year of Jesus.

One can almost hear an echo of Jesus' words, "Will ye also go away?" attending Him wherever He went in that final year. In fact, the echo has never died out, nor should it. Jesus asks us to confirm daily our commitment to serve Him. May it always be, "Lord, to whom shall we go? Thou hast the words of eternal life" (John 6:68).

Lesson 11
Later Galilean Period

By this time the tide of popularity in Christ's ministry had begun to recede because of the message He delivered. This was not surprising since Jesus was telling the people things they did not want to hear. "It was Himself who struck the fatal blow at His popularity."[1] More and more they felt that He was not *their* kind of Messiah.

Jesus saw the stormy skies of opposition lowering fast, and He also knew that the darkest of all days, bringing His death, was not far distant. For six more months He remained in Galilee (the Later Galilean Period of this lesson), fulfilling what is called the Specialized Ministry. This is so called because during this time Jesus generally avoided the public, dealing with such special groups as His twelve disciples, scribes and Pharisees, and Gentiles of northern cities. His major ministry at this time was to instruct His disciples.

A simple way to see the pattern of Jesus' specialized ministry is to recognize the geographical movements. With Capernaum as the natural starting point, He went into the northwest (Tyre and Sidon), then to the southeast (Decapolis region), then to the northeast (Caesarea Philippi). The secret return through Galilee anticipated His journey to Judea.

Study carefully the outline on Chart U, which shows the above pattern. Most of what transpired in III and IV of this outline was intended especially for the benefit of the disciples. Keep this in mind when you study the individual sections. Record in the column entitled DISCIPLES how the twelve were involved in each event. (Note that John does not report this ministry of Jesus' career.)

1. James Stalker, *The Life of Jesus Christ*, rev. ed. (Westwood, N.J.: Revell, 1891), p. 105.

EVENTS	MATTHEW	MARK	LUKE	DISCIPLES
I. TO THE NORTHWEST (Tyre and Sidon)				
1. Dispute over traditions (Capernaum)	15:1-20	7:1-23		
2. To Tyre and Sidon; a daughter healed	15:21-28	7:24-30		
II. TO THE SOUTHEAST (Decapolis)				
—geography reference	15:29a	7:31		
1. Many healings	15:29b-31	7:32-37		
2. Four thousand fed	15:32-39a	8:1-10a		
III. TO THE NORTHEAST (Caesarea Philippi)				
1. Events on the way				
a. near Dalmanutha[2]: dispute with Pharisees and Sadducees	15:39b—16:4a	8:10-12		
b. near Bethsaida: discussion with His disciples	16:4b-12	8:13-21		
c. in Bethsaida: blind man healed		8:22-26		
2. District of Caesarea Philippi				
a. Peter's great confession	16:13-20	8:27-30	9:18-21	
b. Jesus' prophecy of death and resurrection	16:21-28	8:31—9:1	9:22-27	
c. Jesus transfigured	17:1-13	9:2-13	9:28-36	
d. demoniac boy healed	17:14-21	9:14-29	9:37-43a	
IV. SECRET RETURN THROUGH GALILEE				
—disciples are instructed further				
1. Prophecy of death and resurrection	17:22-23	9:30-32	9:43b-45	
2. Tax	17:24-27			
3. Greatness in the kingdom	18:1-35	9:33-50	9:46-50	

2. The location of Dalmanutha (Magdala in Matthew) is still unknown. It may have been on the western shore of the Sea of Galilee.

Three subjects are suggested for special study in this lesson. Be sure to read carefully the biblical text in each case, and answer the questions given. Study of the other parts of this period of Jesus' career should be made as time permits. Follow procedures of study already established in earlier lessons.

I. JESUS AND THE OPPOSITION

The religious leaders were Jesus' main opponents. It was they who eventually stirred up the people to demand Jesus' death. Of the various groups of opponents, the Pharisees were the most antagonistic. Some of the main reasons for rejecting Jesus were: (1) His humble origin; (2) His choice of disciples and company; (3) His spiritual interpretation of rites and holidays, such as fasts, washings, and the Sabbath; and (4) His bold claim to messiahship. Some vital truths that Jesus gave His challengers during this Later Galilean Period concerned:

A. Real Spiritual Defilement (Matt. 15:1-20; Mark 7:1-23)

1. What was Jesus' main point here?

_____

_____

B. Sign of Authority (Matt. 15:39*b*-16:4*a*; Mark 8:10-12)

1. What was the sign of Jonah?

_____

Compare these other references: Matthew 12:38-39; Luke 11:29-30; John 2:18-22.
2. In what ways was the resurrection the key sign? (Cf. Rom. 10:9.)

_____

_____

_____

II. JESUS AND THE GENTILES (Matt. 15:21-28; Mark 7:24-30)

Jesus told the Syrophoenician woman, a Gentile, that His main ministry was to the house of Israel (Matt. 15:24). This was because the divine plan called for raising up a saved people of the Jews and then through them reaching the Gentiles. (Read John 4:21-23.)

As it turned out, Israel by and large rejected the gospel, and there-fore God's witnesses turned to the Gentiles with this message of hope (cf. Rom. 11:11).

1. How did Jesus prove to the woman that the general plan of God regarding a ministry to Jews at that time did not rule out special ministries to Gentiles?

_____

_____

2. What does this passage teach about the woman's faith?

_____

_____

_____

III. JESUS AND THE TWELVE

Most of your study in this lesson should center on Jesus' ministry to the twelve, for that was His main burden during these months. Four highlights are:

A. Peter's Great Confession (Matt. 16:13-20; Mark 8:27-30; Luke 9:18-21)

This is the turning point in Christ's public ministry. We have seen that everything He kept saying and doing was with the main pur-pose of getting people to learn WHO HE WAS.

1. Now, with most of His public ministry behind Him, He asked the key question. What was that question?

_____

_____

2. What was the answer?

_____

3. Had Jesus failed in His ministry?

_____

Note that He quickly directed the same question to the twelve, who were represented by Peter. Study carefully Peter's answer and Jesus' comments.

B. Jesus' Prophecy of Death and Resurrection (Matt. 16:21-28; Mark 8:31–9:1; Luke 9:22-27)

1. "From that time on" Jesus began to tell His disciples clearly and explicitly that He would die and rise again. How do you account for the fact that they would not accept this or believe it?

_____

_____

Note how Jesus begins to involve the disciples intimately with the cross life. Imagine the conflicts and questions rising in the disciples' hearts at this time. Note that Jesus did not end this conversation without identifying Himself with future glory and a kingdom.
2. What are the two aspects of Christian living today with regard to one's fellowship with Christ? (See Phil. 3:10.)

_____

_____

_____

C. Jesus Transfigured (Matt. 17:1-13; Mark 9:2-13; Luke 9:28-36)

This transfiguration has been called by L. S. Chafer a "preview of the coming kingdom on earth" because of the verse immediately preceding the story in each of the three gospels.
1. How was this event intended to benefit the disciples?

_____

_____

2. In what way was it a heartening experience for Jesus, in view of when it took place?

_____

_____

3. What group did Moses represent?

_____

Elijah?

_____

4. How was Jesus related to these?

_____

5. In what ways is Jesus shown to be the key Person here?

_____

_____

_____

6. On what other occasion had the Father's commendation of Matthew 17:5 been made?

_____

7. List some key phrases in this story that stand out to you, and derive some spiritual applications from them.

_____

_____

_____

_____

_____

D. Greatness in the Kingdom (Matt. 18:1-35; Mark 9:33-50; Luke 9:46-50)

In these discourses to His disciples Jesus had in mind mainly their relationships to each other and to the world about them. Jesus was well aware of the many kinds of problems that would attend any witness of the gospel by a group or fellowship, and so He gave practical advice for such situations. Study carefully what is said about each problem listed below. Show how these same problems plague the church today.

Jealousy

_____

Pride

_____

Exclusive cliques

_____

Stumbling block to children

_____

Neglect of the small harvest field

_____

82

An unforgiving spirit

IV. SUMMARY

While Jesus journeyed secretly with His twelve disciples from the northern district around Caesarea Philippi to Capernaum, they marveled at all the different miracles He had performed in their presence. But Jesus was more concerned that they recognize that His miracle-working ministry for all practical purposes was coming to a close:

> Let these teachings sink into your ears:
> The Son of Man is to be delivered into human hands.
> (Luke 9:44, Berkeley)

However, they did not understand what Jesus really meant by this, and they were afraid to inquire.

Such was the determination of Jesus and the clouded allegiance of the disciples as they prepared to leave Galilee for Judea. In six months Jesus would be hanging on the cross for the sins of the world, and these, His closest disciples, would be hiding, ashamed to be identified with Him in any way.

Lesson 12

Later Judean
and Perean Periods

Jesus' Galilean ministry was completed; now He had an appointment with death, resurrection, and ascension. But until the hour to surrender to the enemy was fully come (six months thence), He would minister to towns and villages of Judea and Perea, as well as to the multitudes gathered at Jerusalem for the feasts. This part of Christ's public ministry is called Concluding Ministries, composing the two three-month periods known as Later Judean and Perean. Chart V, excerpted from Chart J, should be familiar to you by now.

RELATIONSHIP OF CONCLUDING MINISTRIES   **Chart V**

FIRST YEAR		SECOND YEAR		THIRD YEAR		
Obscurity		Popularity		Opposition		
opening events	early ministries	extended ministries		specialized ministry	concluding ministries	
—	EARLY JUDEAN	EARLY GALILEAN	MIDDLE GALILEAN	LATER GALILEAN	LATER JUDEAN	PEREAN

                                                        THIS LESSON

Chart W shows the Concluding Ministries Period in amplified form. Keep this survey in mind as you proceed with your studies of this lesson, for proper perspective.

Observe the following facts indicated on Chart W:

1. *Time element.* The Later Judean and Perean periods were each three months long. The annual Feast of Tabernacles and

LATER JUDEAN PERIOD		3 months	PEREAN PERIOD		3 months
PART ONE (1 week)	PART TWO (2 months)	PART THREE (1 week)	PART ONE	INTERRUPTION (brief interval)	PART TWO
Jerusalem Feast of Tabernacles	Regions of Judea	Jerusalem Feast of Dedication	Regions of Perea	Bethany	Regions of Perea
Jesus and Jewish Rulers	Evangelism (Special tour of the 70)	Jesus and Jewish Rulers	Evangelism	Miracle	Evangelism

Feast of Dedication[1] marked the beginning and close of the Later Judean Period. In between, for about two months, the seventy disciples traveled around Judea.

2. *Ministries.* Jesus did evangelistic work in towns and villages of both Judea and Perea, but regarding Judea special attention is called to the evangelistic tour of the seventy. During both periods Jesus spent much of His time in discussions with the Jewish rulers and teaching the multitudes, occasionally performing miracles.

3. *Geography.* Jesus' ministry in Perea was interrupted, of His own choice, by a trip to Judea to raise Lazarus from the dead. (Before going any further in the lesson, review your Palestine geography. Be sure you know the locations of the areas of Judea, Samaria, and Perea, and such cities as Jerusalem, Bethany, Jericho, and Ephraim.)[2]

The following outlines, showing the passages to be read, will help you associate the various events of the two periods with their immediate and distant settings. As you read your Bible, do the following:

1. Record on the chart prominent items called for, such as teachings by Jesus, miracles wrought, reactions of people and the disciples, and identifications of Jesus.

2. Record other observations on another sheet of paper for further study. For example, as you proceed from event to event in Jesus' life, determine what its record contributes to the total story of Jesus.

1. The Feast of Dedication, held for eight days beginning Dec. 25, was not carried over from the Old Testament. It was the anniversary of the rededication of the Temple by the Maccabees in 164 B.C.
2. The Ephraim of John 11:54 was located about twelve miles north of Jerusalem.

Part One	Part Two	Part Three
From Galilee to Jerusalem John 7:2-13 Luke 9:51-62 Matt. 8:19-22	Evangelistic Mission in Judea by the Seventy 1. Sent out Luke 10:1-16 Matt. 10:1-42 2. Return Luke 10:17-24	

JOHN 7:2   JOHN 10:21   JOHN 10:22   JOHN 10:39

FEAST OF TABERNACLES OCT. 15 1 week OCT. 22	2 months	FEAST OF DEDICATION DEC. 25 1 week JAN. 1

Confrontations of Jesus and the Jewish Rulers

Discourses of Jesus

John 7:14—10:21	Luke 10:25—13:21	John 10:22-39
1. In the Midst of Feast 7:14-36	TEACHINGS	
TEACHINGS	10:25:37 38-42	TEACHINGS
REACTIONS	11: 1-13 14-36 37-54	
2. Last day of Feast 7:37—8:59		
TEACHINGS	12:1-12 13-21	
REACTIONS	22-34 35-53 54-59	REACTIONS
3. After the Feast 9:1—10:21		
MIRACLE	13:1-9	
TEACHINGS	10-21	
REACTIONS		

86

3. List spiritual lessons taught by the passages.

QUESTIONS AND OBSERVATIONS

A. Relating to Chart X

1. Why was Jesus' *teaching* ministry more prominent than *healing* at this time?

_____

_____

_____

2. Observe from Luke 10:1 that Jesus also involved Himself with the mission of the seventy.

B. Relating to Chart Y

1. Jesus went to Perea ("beyond Jordan," John 10:40) after the Feast of Dedication, which ended January 1. He arrived back at Bethany, which would be His "home" place[3] till His death, six days before the Passover (John 12:1), or April 8. Thus the Perean ministry lasted about three months.
2. Look for the main teaching of each of the parables of Luke 14:25–16:31.
3. In the middle of His Perean tour Jesus was called back to Bethany because of Lazarus's condition. After He raised Lazarus from the dead, He returned to Perea, via (1) Ephraim, where He was secluded from people (John 11:54), and (2) Samaria and Galilee (Luke 17:11).

A CONCLUDING EXERCISE

The last memorable experience of Jesus before He made His "triumphal" entry into the holy city was the anointing of His feet by Mary of Bethany.[4] Read the narrative again (Matt. 26:6-13; Mark 14:3-9; John 12:1-11). Visualize the setting and action at the supper. Try to imagine what thoughts were Jesus' concerning the following people during the hours that followed:

1. Simon the leper—a reminder of the healing ministry that Jesus had performed for thousands of distressed people

3. Jesus was guest of Mary, Martha, and Lazarus during these days.
4. The chronological placing of this event *before* the entry into Jerusalem is based on John's time reference in 12:1.

John 10:39-40

Evangelistic Mission in Perea by Jesus
(John 10:39-42; Luke 13:22)

John 12:1

JAN. 2	3 months	APRIL 8

Part One	Interruption	Part Two

1. Jesus and the Pharisees
  Luke 13:23—14:24
	The Lazarus Event
	  John 11:1-46
		1. To Perea
		  Luke 17:11—18:14

TEACHINGS	TEACHINGS	HEALING
		TEACHINGS
REACTIONS	REACTIONS	

		2. Through Perea
		  Matt. 19:1—20:28
		  Mark 10:1-45
		  Luke 18:15-34

2. Jesus and the multitudes
  Luke 14:25—16:31
	Jesus in Hiding
	  John 11:47-54
		HEALING

TEACHINGS		TEACHINGS
14:25-35		
15:1-7		

8-10	REACTIONS AND PLOTS	3. To Bethany
		  Matt. 20:29-34
		  Mark 10:46; 14:3-9
		  Luke 18:35—19:28
		  John 11:55—12:11

11-32		
16:1-18		
19-31		HEALING
		TEACHINGS
3. Jesus and His disciples Luke 17:1-10		REACTIONS
TEACHINGS		

2. Lazarus—so recently raised from the dead

3. Martha and Mary—"Lord, if you had been here, my brother would not have died" (John 11:21, Berkeley; cf. v. 32)

4. Judas Iscariot—whom Jesus knew would betray Him

5. The other disciples—"Why this waste?" (Matt. 26:8, Berkeley)

6. Poor people—"The poor you have always with you" (John 12:8, Berkeley)

7. Great crowd of Jews—curious onlookers (John 12:9)

8. Many other Jews—believing in Jesus (John 12:11)

9. Chief priests—planning Jesus' death and Lazarus's death (John 12:10)

Here were poor people, sick people, healed ones, friends and disciples, curious crowds, believing Jews, and murderous rulers. Jesus had ministered to all. Jesus had *given* Himself to all. How much had He *received* from these? Project your answer alongside of these tender words of Jesus concerning Mary's anointing—"She has done a beautiful thing to me" (Matt. 26:10, RSV*) —and you will sense something of the pathos of this final scene before the Passion Week.

Revised Standard Version.

Lesson 13
Passion Week

" "The son of man came not to be ministered unto but to minister, and to give his life a ransom for many." That is how Mark, in his usual compact style, described the purpose of Christ's incarnation (Mark 10:45). The gospels show us that Jesus' public ministry lasted for about three and one-half years. The last week of that ministry, referred to now as Passion Week, was one of conflict, turmoil, and violence, climaxing in the great sacrifice when Jesus "gave up his spirit" while He hung on the cross.

The gospels devote much of their space to Passion Week, or the Sacrifice Period of Jesus' life. (The biblical record of this week, up to the crucifixion, takes up one-third of Matthew and John, one-fourth of Mark, and one-seventh of Luke.) This is because of the week's importance. That was the week for which Jesus was born. Everything else He did and said led up to this and found its meaning in it. The cross was the crucial experience for Christ, because death and Satan were conquered in it. Jesus' crown was made possible by the cross.

The multitudes of Jews attending the Passover when Jesus was crucified were either onlookers or participants in the drama of Golgotha. At that time no one, not even Jesus' close friends and disciples, knew as much about the facts and significance of His death as we do now. The gospels tell the true story and offer the right explanation. The spiritual fervor with which we study this narrative of Passion Week will be a fair indication of how much we really cherish having this inspired Scripture.

The Bible passages involved in this lesson are longer than those of earlier lessons because of the prominence of Passion Week in the four gospels. It is recommended that you divide the lesson into smaller units of study (e.g., each day of Passion Week could be one unit). Take for any one study unit no more than what you can study carefully and adequately.

Some study questions and suggestions are given in this lesson. Most of your study, however, will be on your own. Follow study procedures suggested in earlier lessons, as to types of observations, ways of recording these, sound interpretations, and spiritual applications.

The last week of Jesus' public ministry began on a Sunday when Jesus rode into Jerusalem on a colt, and ended Friday evening when He was crucified. Each day was different from the previous one. Before you begin to read the Bible passages, study Chart Z, which shows general aspects of the week's events. Then as you read the gospels in the order of the extended outlines shown in the next pages, keep in mind this general schedule of the week.

PASSION WEEK   **Chart Z**

KING   KING
EXTOLLED   MOCKED

MINISTRY TO PUBLIC Luke 21:37-38			MINISTRY TO DISCIPLES		SOLITARY MINISTRY
SUN.	MON.	TUES.	WED.	THURS.	FRI.
ACTIVE DAYS			QUIET DAYS		VIOLENT DAYS
authority			compassion		submission
Jesus speaks much					Jesus speaks little

RIDING   DRIVEN OUT
INTO THE CITY   OF THE CITY
ON A COLT   BEARING A CROSS
(Luke 19:35-37)   (John 19:17)

On the first three days, Sunday to Tuesday, Jesus ministered mainly to the multitudes who gathered around the Temple area (Luke 21:37-38). These were active days when Jesus was declaring His *authority* in His last verbal controversies with the religious rulers.

The next two days, Wednesday and Thursday, were quiet days when the Master spent the time mainly with His close disciples and friends, preparing them for the awful event to come. Jesus' *compassion* is prominent here.

Chart AA will help you study the events in sequence. As you study each event, look for main truths, such as:

1. A ministry of Jesus
2. The ones ministered to
3. Identifications of *who Jesus is*
4. Reactions of people

91

	Events	REFERENCES				Identi-fications of Jesus	Reactions to Jesus
		Matthew	Mark	Luke	John		
ACTIVE DAYS — MINISTRY TO THE PUBLIC	SUNDAY Day of Demonstration Triumphal entry into Jerusalem	21:1-11	11:1-11	19:19-44	12:12-19		
	MONDAY Day of Authority Cursing of the fig tree Second cleansing of the Temple	21:18-19 12-17	11:12-14 15-19	 19:45-48			
	TUESDAY Day of Conflict Fig tree withered Christ's authority challenged Three parables of warning Three "catch" questions Jesus challenges the rulers Other discourses of Jesus Prophetic discourses Betrayal offer of Judas	21:20-22 23-27 28-32 33-46 22:1-14 15-22 23-33 34-40 41-46 23:1-12 13-36 37-39 24—25 26:3-5, 14-16	11:20-26 27-33 12:1-12 13-17 18-27 28-34 35-37 38-40 41-44 13 14:1-2, 10-11	 20:1-8 9-19 20-26 27-39 27-40 41-44 45-47 21:1-4 5-36 22:1-2, 3-6	 12:20-50		
QUIET DAYS — MINISTRY TO THE DISCIPLES	WEDNESDAY Day of Rest —no events recorded in the gospels —probably time was spent by Jesus and His disciples in rest and instruction —enemies were probably further plotting Jesus' death						
	THURSDAY Day of Preparation Paschal supper Foot washing Lord's Supper Farewell discourses Intercessory prayer	26:17-25 26-29 31-35	14:12-21 22-25 27-31	22:7-18, 21-30 19-20 31-38	13:18-30 1-17 13:33— 16:33 17		

92

PASSION WEEK

Events	REFERENCES				Identi-fications of Jesus	Opposition to Jesus
	Matthew	Mark	Luke	John		
FRIDAY Day of Suffering Midnight to 2 A.M., Gethsemane, prayer, betrayal, arrest	26:30, 36-56	14:26, 32-52	22:39-54	18:1-12		
3 to 5 a.m., Trials Before Jewish Authorities (Religious)						
1. Annas (high priest emeritus)				18:13-23		
2. Caiaphas (ruling high priest)	26:57-68	14:53-65	22:54, 63-65	24		
(denials of Peter)	69-75	66-72	55-62	25-27		
3. Sanhedrin (suicide of Judas)	27:1 3-10	15:1a	66-71			
6 a.m. to 9 a.m., Trials Before Roman Authorities (Civil)		15:1b-5	23:1-6	18:28-38		
1. Pilate	27:2, 11-14		7-12			
2. Herod			13-25	18:39— 19:16		
3. Pilate	15-26	6-15				
(mockery by soldiers)	27-31	16-20				
9 a.m. to 3 p.m. Crucifixion	27:31b-49	15:20b-36	23:26-45	19:17-29		
Death	50-56	37-41	46-49	30-37		
Before Sunset Burial	27:57-60	15:42-46	23:50-54	19:38-42		

5. key words and phrases
6. Training of the disciples
7. Truths taught about the death of Christ
8. Truths taught about salvation
9. The world and power of Satan
10. Jesus' prophecies of resurrection and victory

Space has been left on Chart AA for you to briefly record identifications of Jesus (whether by the people, rulers, disciples, or Jesus Himself) and reactions to Jesus.

Friday was D-day for Jesus' enemies, the day scheduled for His arrest, trial, and death. Friday differed from the days preceding it. The first three days were active ones when Jesus declared His authority to the multitudes; the next two days were quiet ones for Jesus when He ministered to His disciples, unfolding a heart of compassion; this last day, Friday, was a day of violence by the hosts of darkness when they took Christ the Lamb, the quiet, submissive One, the lonely, forsaken One, and slew Him.

There was no sleep for Jesus Thursday night. The hours until midnight were spent in prayer, and then in that dark hour, and unobserved by the multitudes, many of whom might have objected, the enemies came and arrested Him.

The reason for the two trials is apparent. Rome ruled Palestine, but a measure of home rule was allowed the local Jewish government in the land, subject to the approval of the Roman authorities. The crime of which Jesus was accused by the Jews—blasphemy—was of an ecclesiastical nature, and so the case was tried before Jewish authorities—the high priest and Sanhedrin (court). The court gave the death sentence; but since only the Roman civil powers could carry out such a sentence, Jesus was referred to Judea's governor, Pilate, and to King Herod who had jurisdiction over Galilee, of which Jesus was a native.

I. OBSERVATIONS AND QUESTIONS ON SELECTED PORTIONS

Sunday

1. Why is this entry of Jesus into Jerusalem called "triumphal"?

_____

_____

2. Compare Zechariah 9:9-10; Mark 11:9-10; Luke 19:38; and Matthew 21:11 as to recognitions of Jesus.

_____

_____

_____

Monday

1. What is perfect praise? (Matt. 21:16; cf. Ps. 8:2)

_____

Tuesday

1. *Parables of warning.* Note how specific and strong were Jesus' warnings of judgment to come. Should Christians today include judgment warning in the gospel message?

_____

2. *"Catch questions."* Identify the group that challenged Jesus each time. What did the religionists lack to be unable to answer their own questions?

_____

_____

_____

3. *Jesus' challenges.* What various sins of the religious leaders did Jesus expose here?

_____

_____

_____

4. *Prophetic discourses.* These discourses were brought on when the disciples remarked to Jesus about the wonderful Temple buildings. When Jesus foretold the Temple's destruction, the disciples asked a threefold question: (1) When will this be? (2) What will be the sign of Your coming? (3) What will be the sign of the close of the age? (Matt. 24:3). Parts of this "Olivet Discourse" are difficult to interpret, and you may want to consult a commentary for help. The main truths to learn here are those concerning the second coming of Christ, whether they are taught in symbol, by illustration, or explicitly. In the beginning of His discourse Jesus spoke about false alarms and true signs (e.g., Matt. 24:4-31). Verses 4-22 probably foretold the destruction of Jerusalem in A.D. 70, in answer to the disciples' first question. At the same time these verses furnished illustrations of the signs of the times of Jesus' second coming, which verses 23-31 more explicitly described. In the remainder of the discourse, Jesus gave practical exhortations and warnings, mostly by way of parables, emphasizing the imminence of His return and the need of being always ready to meet Him. As you study this discourse, list the many practical lessons Jesus taught that are so vital to Christian living today.

Wednesday

The gospels are silent concerning this day.

Thursday

Stalker says this of Thursday evening: "It was the greatest evening in His life. His soul overflowed in indescribable tenderness and grandeur."[1]

1. *Foot washing*. What is the main spiritual lesson of this event?

_____

_____

2. *The Lord's Supper*. What various truths are taught by this ordinance? (Cf. 1 Cor. 11:23-26.)

_____

_____

3. *Farewell discourses*. Make a list of all the wonderful truths spoken by Jesus in these discourses.

_____

_____

_____

_____

4. *Intercessory prayer*. John 17 is the classic chapter on the great high priestly prayer of Jesus. Study it carefully and meditate much on these intimate words of the Son to His Father. Why must this communion with His Father have been a heartening experience for Jesus at this time?

_____

Friday

1. Try to identify the various causes of Jesus' agony, in the total picture.

_____

_____

2. What pattern do you see in the trials?

_____

_____

1. James Stalker, *The Life of Jesus Christ*, rev. ed. (Westwood, N.J.: Revell, 1891), p. 125.

96

Note the absence of justice. Account for Jesus' relative silence.

_____

_____

3. Compare (1) denials of Peter, (2) suicide of Judas, (3) mockery of the soldiers. Compare especially the hearts of the men involved.
4. Study the seven last "words" of Jesus in their respective contexts, keeping in mind that these were spoken during the agonizing hours of the most cruel torture imaginable. Stalker comments that these words are seven windows through which we can see the heart and mind of Jesus. "They show that He retained unimpaired the serenity and majesty which had characterized Him throughout His trial. . . . "[2]

> *Spoken from 9:00 A.M.-12:00 M.*
> "Father, forgive them" (Luke 23:34).
> "To day shalt thou be with me in paradise" (Luke 23:43).
> "Woman, behold thy son" (John 19:26).
> *Spoken from 12:00 M.-3:00 P.M.*
> "My God, my God . . . " (Matt. 27:46; Mark 15:34).
> "I thirst" (John 19:28).
> "It is finished" (John 19:30).
> "Father, into thy hands I commend my spirit" (Luke 23:46).

5. Excruciating pain and intolerable thirst were two of the physical tortures of crucifixion. But Jesus' greater agony was of mind and heart.

> He whose very life was love, who thirsted for love as the hart pants for the water-brooks, was encircled with a sea of hatred and of dark, bitter, hellish passion, that surged round Him and flung up its waves about His cross. His soul was spotlessly pure . . . but sin pressed itself against it, endeavoring to force upon it its loathsome contact, from which it shrank through every fiber.[3]

6. Consult a Bible dictionary or encyclopedia for a description of the Roman punishments of scourging and crucifixion.

2. Ibid., p. 143
3. Ibid., p. 144

CONCLUDING EXERCISE

You have now studied the historical record of Jesus' death. Before moving on to the next chapter about His resurrection, tarry long over the following questions, which look for the deeper *meaning* of Christ's death.

1. Why did Jesus die?

_____

_____

2. If Jesus gave His life a ransom for *all*, will all be saved?

_____

What condition for salvation, imposed on the sinner, is related to His death?

_____

_____

3. Would Jesus' death have lost its efficacy if His body had remained in the tomb? If so, why?

_____

_____

4. What made Jesus an adequate substitutionary sacrifice for us?

_____

_____

5. What does Jesus' death have to do with the cross life of the Christian today?

_____

_____

Lesson 14
The Resurrected Christ

Jesus' disciples had seen their master in every conceivable type of ministry, symbolized by various posture images. These even come to our mind today as we think of Him. Jesus walked straight and tall, as an example of righteous living. He bent over to serve, and He kneeled to pray. He looked out across the masses in compassion and raised His eyes to heaven in hope. He raised His hands as He taught, and He pointed His finger as He judged. He sat with sinners to witness, and He walked with His disciples in fellowship.

And then He hung on the cross, and His body was laid out in a tomb. Was that to be the last memory for the disciples?

> There never was an enterprise in the world which seemed more completely at an end than did that of Jesus on the last Old Testament Sabbath. . . . When He was buried, there was not a single human being that believed He would ever rise again before the day of the world's doom.[1]

The disciples had known some wonderfully bright days in the past, walking with Jesus. But they did not know in this hour of utter darkness, with Christ dead, that the brightest day was yet to come. Resurrection day was on God's blueprint even though no disciple gave it a thought.

There can be no Easter faith without Easter fact. On the fact of the resurrection of Christ's literal body hangs the truth of the gospel's message of salvation and the Christian religion. The main emphasis of the study of this lesson will be to observe the fact-

1. James Stalker, *The Life of Jesus Christ*, rev. ed. (Westwood, N.J.: Revell, 1891), p. 146.

uality of the resurrection and thus see the keynote of the gospel that the resurrection proclaims.

I. THE EVENT OF THE RESURRECTION

A. Facts Surrounding the Event

The gospels are silent concerning the exact moment and manner of Christ's resurrection. True of all miracles, the grand miracle defies full description and natural explanation. In recording the events that were sequels to the miracle, the gospels have established its historicity. The first sequel was the angel's rolling back the tomb's stone, intended not to let Jesus out but to let witnesses in. Outlined in Chart BB is a schedule of events from Jesus' cruci-

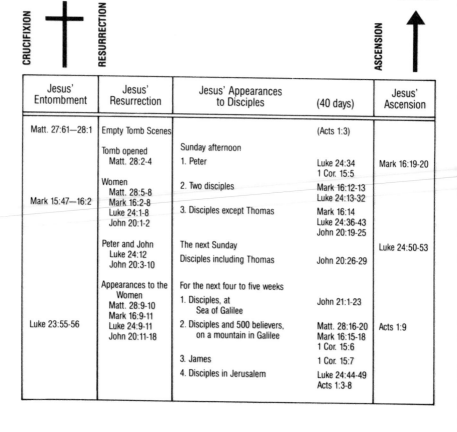

POSTRESURRECTION APPEARANCES   **Chart BB**

Jesus' Entombment	Jesus' Resurrection	Jesus' Appearances to Disciples	(40 days)	Jesus' Ascension
Matt. 27:61—28:1	Empty Tomb Scenes		(Acts 1:3)	
	Tomb opened Matt. 28:2-4	Sunday afternoon 1. Peter	Luke 24:34 1 Cor. 15:5	Mark 16:19-20
Mark 15:47—16:2	Women Matt. 28:5-8 Mark 16:2-8 Luke 24:1-8 John 20:1-2	2. Two disciples 3. Disciples except Thomas	Mark 16:12-13 Luke 24:13-32 Mark 16:14 Luke 24:36-43 John 20:19-25	
	Peter and John Luke 24:12 John 20:3-10	The next Sunday Disciples including Thomas	John 20:26-29	Luke 24:50-53

Luke 23:55-56	Appearances to the Women
	Matt. 28:9-10
	Mark 16:9-11
	Luke 24:9-11
	John 20:11-18
		For the next four to five weeks
		1. Disciples, at
		   Sea of Galilee
		2. Disciples and 500 believers,
		   on a mountain in Galilee
		
		3. James
		4. Disciples in Jerusalem
			John 21:1-23
			
			Matt. 28:16-20
			Mark 16:15-18
			1 Cor. 15:6
			1 Cor. 15:7
			Luke 24:44-49
			Acts 1:3-8
				Acts 1:9

fixion to His ascension, as recorded by the gospels. As you read the passages, record your own observations on another paper.

B. Authentication of the Facts

Because the gospel message depends on the truth of the resurrection of Jesus' body, God gave authentication of the event in various incontestable ways. Those who deny such proof are those who do not want to know the truth.

The following list shows various authentications of the resurrection.[2] Read each Bible passage, and note the strength of the witness.

1. Open tomb (John 20:1-2)
2. Recovered graveclothes (John 20:3-8)
3. Appearances of the risen Lord (studied earlier in this lesson)
4. Pilate's orders to seal and guard the tomb (Matt. 27:62-66)
5. Removal of the stone by an angel (Matt.28:1-3)
6. Terror of the Roman guards (Matt.28:4)
7. Message of the angel to the women (Matt.28:5-6)
8. Report of the guards to the chief priests (Matt. 28:11)
9. Chief priests' bribe to the Roman guards (Matt. 28:12-13)
10. Lie spread by the Roman guards (Matt. 28:15)
11. Certainty of Christ's death (John 19:34-42)
12. Certainty of Christ's burial (Mark 15:42-47)
13. Certainty that Christ's body was not stolen (cf. Matt. 28:4-15)
14. Changed lives of the disciples
15. Conversions like that of Saul of Tarsus
16. Two-thousand-year witness of the Christian church and the holy Scriptures

II. THE GOSPEL OF THE RESURRECTION

The books of the New Testament that follow the gospels are saturated with the key truth of Christ's resurrection. Some of the main passages referring to this event are listed below. Read each passage, and record opposite the reference what it teaches about the resurrection. Make personal applications whenever possible.

Acts 2:24, 32-33 _____

3:15, 26 _____

4:2, 10 _____

2. Taken in part from *Unger's Bible Handbook* (Chicago: Moody, 1966), pp. 564-65.

Acts 5:31   _____

    10:40-41   _____

    13:30-37   _____

    17:31   _____

Romans 4:24-25   _____

    5:8-10   _____

    6:4, 9   _____

    7:4   _____

    8:11, 34   _____

    10:9   _____

1 Corinthians 6:14   _____

        15:1-58   _____

2 Corinthians 4:14   _____

Galatians 1:1   _____

Ephesians 1:18-22 _____

    4:8-13   _____

Philippians 3:10   _____

Colossians 2:12   _____

1 Thessalonians 1:10 _____

        4:14   _____

1 Timothy 2:5-6   _____

2 Timothy 2:8   _____

1 Peter 1:3, 21   _____

After you have studied the above passages, state in your own words how each of the following depends on Christ's resurrection:

1. Efficacy of the atoning blood of Christ

_____

_____

2. Fellowship with God

_____

_____

3. Conquest of the fear of death and judgment

_____

_____

4. Assurance of the truth of God's promises

_____

_____

5. Real existence of believers in heaven

_____

_____

III. CHRIST'S ASCENSION

Read again the passages of the ascension shown earlier in this lesson.

Jesus tarried on this earth forty days after His resurrection, long enough to give ample proof that He had conquered death and the grave. That provided assurance and joy for the disciples. But what about power to fulfill His commission (Luke 24:48; Acts 1:8)? For this, the Holy Spirit would be sent (Acts 1:8); and while the disciples were faithfully waiting for that enduement, He came down and filled the hearts of the apostles. With this, the dawning of a new day for the world had arrived. We are still in that day, but night is fast approaching. As Christians we may well ask ourselves this personal question: "How faithful are we in our witness, by life and word, to the gospel of the risen Christ?"

IV. CHRIST'S CONTINUING MINISTRY

Since the main purpose of this manual is to study the life of Christ on earth as this story is told by the gospels, only this brief reference will be made to His important continuing ministry. That ministry is taught mainly by the epistles and Revelation. (Other books of this study series treat this subject in detail.)

During Jesus' public ministry, He served as a *Prophet,* proclaiming a message of redemption to lost sinners. Now, seated at the right hand of the Father, He serves mainly as the believer's *Priest,* interceding for him before the Father. At some future date

He shall return to this earth in the role of *Judge* and of *King*, ushering in a sequence of events that will climax in a consummation of eternal woe for unbelievers (Rev. 20:7-15) and eternal bliss for believers (Rev. 21:1–22:5).

Believers can voice with John the thrilling expectation and prayer concerning Christ's soon return: "Even so, come, Lord Jesus" (Rev.22:21).

Lesson 15
A Concluding Study

Certain elements took prominence in the multifaceted ministry Jesus performed before the multitudes. Three of these are His parables, miracles, and use of Scripture. In this concluding lesson we will look at each of these briefly and then will formulate a summary of the basic message He delivered to His audiences.

I. PARABLES OF JESUS[1]

A. Definition

A parable is the recounting of a common incident from daily life in concise, figurative form to illustrate a spiritual truth.

B. Purposes

Jesus taught parables mainly to the unbelieving multitudes (cf. Matt. 13:1-3, 10). From Matthew 13:10-17 it appears that Jesus had two purposes in using parables with unbelievers: (1) to arouse interest and teach them basic truths, so that they would want to hear more; and (2) to withhold the deeper mysteries from them, reserving those for believers, who would receive such truths.

---

1. For an extensive treatment of this subject, consult G. Campbell Morgan, *The Parables and Metaphors of Our Lord* (Westwood, N.J.: Revell, 1943), and Richard C. Trench, *Notes on the Parables of Our Lord* (Westwood, N.J.: Revell, 1948).

C. Principles of Interpretation

What Jesus meant to teach by a parable is the interpretation of the parable. Here are a few basic principles of interpretation that will help you analyze any parable:

1. Look for the primary intent of the parable.
2. Interpret any subordinate detail of the parable in light of this main intent.
3. Note that not all details have a spiritual meaning.
4. Remember that the context of the parable is its best interpreter
   (a) What occasion brought on the parable?
   (b) To whom was the parable addressed?
   (c) What was the effect of teaching the parable?
   (d) How did Jesus interpret the parable, if He did?
5. The cultural background of the parable must be recognized.
6. The parables were spoken during the transition period from the old covenant to the new, and should be so recognized.
7. Doctrines are not established in parables; they are illustrated by them.

D. List of Parables

Below are listed the parables of Jesus according to groups.[2] Various kinds of studies may be made in the parables. The above principles of interpretation will suggest various approaches.

  I. Didactic Parables
    A. Nature and Development of the Kingdom
      1. The Sown Seed (Matt. 13:3-8; Mark 4:4-8; Luke 8:5-8)
      2. The Tares (Matt. 13:24-30)
      3. The Mustard Seed (Matt. 13:31-32; Mark 4:30-32; Luke 13:18-19)
      4. The Leaven (Matt. 13:33; Luke 13:20-21)
      5. The Hidden Treasure (Matt. 13:44)
      6. The Pearl of Great Price (Matt. 13:45-46)
      7. The Dragnet (Matt. 13:47-50)
      8. The Blade, the Ear, and the Full Corn (Mark 4:26-29)
    B. Service and Rewards
      1. The Laborers in the Vineyard (Matt. 20:1-16)
      2. The Talents (Matt. 25:14-30)
      3. The Pounds (Luke 19:11-27)

---

2. This list, adapted from A.B. Bruce, *The Parabolic Teaching of Christ* (London: Hodder & Stoughton, 1904), appears in Merrill C. Tenney, ed., *The Zondervan Pictorial Bible Dictionary* (Grand Rapids: Zondervan, 1963), p. 622.

4. The Unprofitable Servant (Luke 17:7-10)
C. Prayer
   1. The Friend at Midnight (Luke 11:5-8)
   2. The Unjust Judge (Luke 18:1-8)
D. Love for Neighbor
   1. The Good Samaritan (Luke 10:30-37)
E. Humility
   1. The Lowest Seat at the Feast (Luke 14:7-11)
   2. The Pharisee and the Publican (Luke 18:9-14)
F. Worldly Wealth
   1. The Unjust Steward (Luke 16:1-9)
   2. The Rich Fool (Luke 12:16-21)
   3. The Great Supper (Luke 14:16-24)
II. Evangelic Parables
A. God's Love for the Lost
   1. The Lost Sheep (Matt. 18:12-14; Luke 15:3-7)
   2. The Lost Coin (Luke 15:8-10)
   3. The Lost Son (Luke 15:11-32)
B. Gratitude of the Redeemed
   1. The Two Debtors (Luke 7:41-43)
III. Prophetic and Judicial Parables
A. Watchfulness for Christ's Return
   1. The Ten Virgins (Matt. 25:1-13)
   2. The Faithful and Unfaithful Servants (Matt. 24:45-51; Luke 12:42-48)
   3. The Watchful Porter (Mark 13:34-37)
B. Judgment on Israel and Within the Kingdom
   1. The Two Sons (Matt. 21:28-32)
   2. The Wicked Husbandmen (Matt. 21:33-34; Mark 12:1-12; Luke 20:9-18)
   3. The Barren Fig Tree (Luke 13:6-9)
   4. The Marriage Feast of the King's Son (Matt. 22:1-14)
   5. The Unforgiving Servant (Matt. 18:23-35)

II. MIRACLES OF JESUS[3]

A. Definition

A miracle is a supernatural event injected into the external world of nature by the immediate power of God. (Note the words "miracles," "wonders," and "signs" in Acts 2:22.)

---

3. Two recommended books on miracles are Richard C. Trench, *Notes on the Miracles of Our Lord* (Westwood, N. J.: Revell, 1948), and C. S. Lewis, *Miracles* (New York: Macmillan, 1947).

B. Purposes

There were two basic purposes of Jesus' miracles. These were revelation and edification.

Revelation

1. To show divine credentials for Jesus and thus authenticate His message (read John 5:36)
2. To symbolize His spiritual and saving work (cf. Luke 5:23)
3. To attract an audience (cf. John 12:9) (Christ's miracles "were only the bell tolled to bring the people to hear his words."[4])

Edification

1. To pour out upon people a measure of the divine fullness (cf. Luke 8:46)
2. To help people in their physical and mental needs

C. Suggestions for Studying Christ's Miracles

When you study a miracle of Christ, look for the following, among other things:

1. What was Christ teaching by performing the miracle?
2. How was Christ revealed in the miracle?
3. Who was the person or group involved in the miracle?
4. What was the need calling forth the miracle?
5. What requisites, such as faith, were necessary?
6. What good effects came of the miracle?

LIST OF MIRACLES

Chart CC

	MATTHEW	MARK	LUKE	JOHN
Feeding of the Five Thousand	14:15-21	6:35-44	9:12-17	6:5-14
Stilling the Tempest	8:23-27	4:35-41	8:22-25	
Demons and the Swine	8:28-34	5:1-20	8:26-39	
Jairus' Daughter Raised	9:18-26	5:22-24, 35-43	8:41-42, 49-56	
Woman with Issue of Blood	9:20-22	5:25-34	8:43-48	
Paralytic at Capernaum	9:1-8	2:1-12	5:17-26	

4. James Stalker, *The Life of Jesus Christ*, rev. ed. (Westwood, N.J.: Revell, 1891), p. 67.

	MATTHEW	MARK	LUKE	JOHN
Leper at Gennesaret	8:1-4	1:40-45	5:12-15	
Peter's Mother-in-Law	8:14-17	1:29-31	4:38-39	
Withered Hand Restored	12:9-13	3:1-5	6:6-11	
Lunatic Child	17:14-21	9:14-29	9:37-42	
Walking on the Sea	14:22-33	6:45-52	6:19-21	
Blind Bartimaeus	20:29-34	10:46-52	18:35-43	
Syrophoenician Girl	15:21-28	7:24-30		
Four Thousand Fed	15:32-39	8:1-9		
Cursing of Fig Tree	21:17-22	11:12-14, 20-24		
Centurion's Servant	8:5-13		7:1-10	
Demoniac Man		1:23-26	4:33-36	
Blind and Dumb Demoniac	12:22		11:14	
Two Blind Men	9:27-31			
Dumb Demoniac	9:32-33			
Shekel in the Fish's Mouth	17:24-27			
Deaf Mute		7:31-37		
Blind Man at Bethsaida		8:22-26		
First Miraculous Draught of Fishes			5:1-11	
Nain Widow's Son Raised			7:11-16	
Woman with Eighteen-year Infirmity			13:10-17	
Man with Dropsy			14:1-6	
Ten Lepers			17:11-19	
Ear of Malchus			22:49-51	
Water into Wine				2:1-11
Nobleman's Son at Cana				4:46-54
Impotent Man at Bethesda				5:1-16
Man Born Blind				9:1-8
Lazarus Raised				11:1-45
Second Miraculous Draught of Fishes				21:1-14

D. List of Miracles

Jesus performed many more miracles than are recorded in the gospels.[5] The thirty-five miracles that are recorded are listed in Chart CC.

III. JESUS' USE OF THE SCRIPTURES

About half the entire content of the gospels are the spoken words of Jesus. Of these, many are quotes of Old Testament verses. In the entire New Testament there are 275 Old Testament quotations, of which a large proportion were spoken by Jesus. Jesus referred to the Scriptures often because they were God's written revelation to man. He used it when talking about fulfillment of prophecy or when He was teaching about the way to God and the walk with God. To Him, it was man's book of light.

Jesus clearly demonstrated what an important help the Scriptures are in daily living by quoting them to Satan in His wilderness temptations (Matt. 4:1-11). Christians today have much to learn from the example of Jesus in using the Bible. A profitable study of the list below would be to observe these aspects of Jesus' use of the Scriptures.

1. The note of authority that Jesus always recognized in the Scriptures

2. The liberties Jesus took in applying timeless principles to contemporary situations

3. How Jesus used the Scriptures to correct error, teach doctrine, rebuke Satan, offer hope, comfort and challenge the believer

OLD TESTAMENT PASSAGES
QUOTED OR ALLUDED TO BY JESUS   Chart DD

Old Testament Verse and Subject	Jesus' Quote			
	Matthew	Mark	Luke	John
Genesis				
1:27; 5:2	19:4	10:6		
2:24	19:5	10:7-8		
4:8	23:35		11:51	
6:11-13	24:37		17:26	
7:7, 21-23	24:37		17:26	

5. Note groups of miracles mentioned in these references: Mark 6:56; Matt. 4:23ff.; 9:35ff.; Luke 4:40ff.; 5:15ff.; 6:17-19; 7:21ff.; John 2:23; 3:2; 4:45; 20:30; 21:25.

Old Testament Verse and Subject	Jesus' Quote			
	Matthew	Mark	Luke	John
17:9-14				7:22
18:14	19:26	10:27		
18:20-22			17:28-32	
19:24	11:24		10:12; 17:28-32	
19:26			17:28-32	
28:12				1:51
38:8			20:28-38	
Exodus				
3:6, 15	22:32	12:26	20:37-38	
20:7	5:33ff.			
20:12; 21:17	15:4; 19:18-19	7:10; 10:19	18:20	
20:13	5:21f.			
20:14	5:27			
21:17		7:10		
21:24	5:38			
22:1			19:8, 10	
24:8	26:28	14:24		
Leviticus				
2:13		9:49		
4:18-20	26:28	14:24		
12:1-3				7:22
13:49		1:44	5:14	
14:2-32		1:44	5:14	
19:12	5:33ff.			
19:18	5:43; 19:19; 22:39			
20:9	15:4	7:10		
24:9	12:3	2:25	6:3	
24:20	5:38			
27:30	23:23		11:42	
Numbers				
5:6-7			19:8, 10	
21:8-9				3:14

Old Testament Verse and Subject	Jesus' Quote			
	Matthew	Mark	Luke	John
28:9-10	12:5			
30:2	5:33ff.			
Deuteronomy				
5:11	5:33ff			
5:16-17	5:21f.	7:10; 10:19	18:20	
5:18	5:27			
5:19-20	19:18			
6:4, 6		12:29		
6:5	22:37			
6:13	4:10		4:8	
6:16	4:7		4:12	
8:3	4:4		4:4	
13:1	24:24			
17:6				8:17
19:15	18:16			8:17
19:21	5:38			
23:3-6	5:43			
23:21	5:33ff.			
24:1	5:31			
25:5			20:28, 38	
25:19	5:43			
1 Samuel				
21:1-6	12:3	2:25	6:3	
1 Kings				
17:1, 8-9			4:25-27	
18:1-2			4:25-27	
19:2, 10	17:11-12			
2 Kings				
5:1, 14			4:27	
2 Chronicles				
24:20-21	23:35		11:51	

Old Testament Verse and Subject	Jesus' Quote			
	Matthew	Mark	Luke	John
Job				
42:2		10:27		
Psalms				
6:8			13:27	
18:25	5:7			
22:1	27:46	15:34		
24:3-5	5:8			
31:5			23:46	
35:19				15:25
37:11	5:5			
41:9		14:18		13:18; 17:12
42:6		14:34		12:27
48:2	5:35			
62:12	16:27	8:38		
82:6				10:34
91:11	4:6			
107:3			13:29	
110:1	22:44; 26:64	12:36; 14:62	20:42f.; 22:69	
118:22	21:42	12:10	20:17	
118:26	23:39	11:9		
Proverbs				
11:17	5:7			
18:4				7:38
Ecclesiastes				
12:2		13:24		
Isaiah				
5:1f.	21:33	12:2	20:9	
6:9-10	13:14-15	4:12; 8:18	8:10	12:40
8:14	21:44		20:18	
13:9-10	24:29-30		21:25f.	
14:13-15	11:23		10:15	

Old Testament Verse and Subject	Jesus' Quote			
	Matthew	Mark	Luke	John
29:13	15:8-9	7:6-7		
35:5-6			7:22	
49:12	8:11		13:29	
53:12			22:37	
54:13				6:45
55:1	5:6			
56:7	21:13	11:17	19:46	
58:6			4:18f.	
61:1f.	11:5		4:18f.; 7:22	
61:2	5:4		6:21	
66:1	5:33ff.			
66:14				16:22
66:24		9:48		
Jeremiah				
5:21		8:18		
6:16	11:29f.			
7:11	21:13	11:17	19:46	
12:7	23:38f.			
22:5	23:38f.			
31:31	26:28	14:24		
Ezekiel				
12:2		8:18		
32:7-8	24:29-30		21:25f.	
34:16			19:8, 10	
34:23				10:16
37:24				10:16
Daniel				
4:9-21	13:32	4:32		
7:13	24:30; 26:64	13:26; 14:62	21:27-28; 22:69	
8:10	24:29	13:24-25	21:25f.	
9:27	24:15	13:14	21:20	

Old Testament Verse and Subject	Jesus' Quote			
	Matthew	Mark	Luke	John
11:31	24:15			
12:1	24:21	13:9	21:22	
12:2	25:46			
12:3	13:43			
12:11	24:15			
Hosea				
6:2			24:46	
6:6	9:13; 12:7			
10:8			23:30	
Joel				
3:13		4:29		
3:15-16	24:29	13:24	21:25f.	
Amos				
8:9	24:29		21:25f.	
Jonah				
1:17; 2:1-2; 3:5; 4:3	12:40		11:32	
3:4	16:4		11:29	
Micah				
6:8	23:23		11:42, 51	
7:6	10:35	13:12	12:53	
Zephaniah				
1:14-16	24:29-30		21:25f.	
Zechariah				
9:11	26:28			
13:7	26:31	14:27		
14:5b	25:31			
Malachi				
3:1	11:10		7:27	
4:5	11:14	9:12		
4:5-6	17:11-12			

The list given in Chart DD may be used as a reference for making various studies of Jesus' use of the Old Testament. It is interesting to observe not only the frequency of His quotes but the variety of books from which He quoted.

IV. THE MESSAGE OF JESUS

God has spoken to man finally, fully, and preeminently by His Son (Heb. 1:1-2). Because Jesus is the Word, He made possible communication between God and man (John 1:1).

The message that Jesus delivered came via the services He rendered, the sacrifice He offered, and the words He spoke. A brief look at the last of these—the words He spoke—may serve as a summary exercise for this study guide.

Jesus taught and preached to people whose basic needs were no different from the needs of all people of all ages. The universal plague on all people is threefold: (1) guilt for *past* sins; (2) perverseness of *present* living; and (3) anxiety over the unknown *future*. Think back over the public ministry of Jesus, and list the various truths He spoke that were directed to these human needs. Record your thoughts, and watch the list grow the more you ponder over His ministry. After you have done this, study the following list of subjects about which Jesus spoke. Add other items to the list. How did these subjects enlighten Jesus' audiences and offer them hope?

---

1. Absolute authority (Who has the first and final word?)
2. Nature of man (What is man like? In whose image was he made?)
3. The Person and work of the Father (How are God's holiness and love a part of the gospel?)
4. The Person and work of the Son (Did Jesus clearly claim to be the Son of God and the Saviour of men?)
5. The law and sin (How are these related?)
6. The kingdom
   (a) Entrance into the kingdom of God (What is the door?)
   (b) Living in the kingdom (Is this possible?)
   (c) Workers in the kingdom (What are Christians' obligations?)
7. Last things (What is the future of this earth and of humankind?)

And now—glory to Him Who alone is God,
Who saves us through Jesus Christ our Lord;
yes, splendor and majesty,
all power and authority
are His from the beginning;
His they are
and His they evermore will be.
And He is able to keep you from slipping and falling away,
and to bring you, sinless and perfect,
into His glorious presence with mighty shouts of
everlasting joy. AMEN.

(Jude 24-25, *The Living Bible*)

Bibliography

RESOURCES FOR FURTHER STUDY

Dowley, Tim. *The Moody Guide to Bible Lands.* Chicago: Moody, 1988.

Everyday Bible. New Testament Study Edition. Minneapolis: World Wide, 1988.

Geisler, Norman L. *Christ: The Theme of the Bible.* Chicago: Moody, 1968.

Lewis, C.S. *Miracles.* New York: Macmillan, 1947.

New International Version Study Bible. Grand Rapids: Zondervan, 1985.

Pfeiffer, C.F., and Harrison, E.F., eds. *The Wycliffe Bible Commentary.* Chicago: Moody, 1962.

Pfeiffer, C.F., and Vos, Howard F. *The Wycliffe Historical Geography of Bible Lands.* Chicago: Moody, 1967.

The Ryrie Study Bible. Chicago: Moody, 1985.

Tenney, Merrill C. *New Testament Times.* Grand Rapids: Eerdmans, 1965.

Tenney, Merrill C., ed. *The Zondervan Pictorial Bible Dictionary.* Grand Rapids: Zondervan, 1963.

Unger, Merrill F. *New Unger's Bible Dictionary.* Chicago: Moody, 1988.

———. *The New Unger's Bible Handbook.* Chicago: Moody, 1984.

Wieand, Albert Cassel. *A New Harmony of the Gospels.* Rev. ed. Grand Rapids: Eerdmans, 1950. Uses the *Revised Standard Version.*

COMMENTARIES AND TOPICAL STUDIES

Andrews, Samuel J. *The Life of Our Lord upon the Earth.* Grand Rapids: Zondervan, 1954.

Edersheim, Alfred. *The Life and Times of Jesus the Messiah.* Rev.ed. 2 vols. Grand Rapids: Eerdmans, 1953.

Morgan, G. Campbell. *The Crises of the Christ.* Westwood, N.J.: Revell, 1936.

_____. *The Parables and Metaphors of Our Lord.* Westwood, N.J.: Revell, 1943.

Robertson, A. T. *A Harmony of the Gospels for Students of the Life of Christ.* New York: Harper, 1922. Uses the *American Standard Version.*

Roney, Charles Patrick. *Commentary on the Harmony of the Gospels.* Grand Rapids: Eerdmans, 1948.

Scroggie, W. Graham. *A Guide to the Gospels.* London: Pickering & Inglis, 1948.

Stalker, James. *The Life of Jesus Christ.* Rev. ed. Westwood, N.J.: Revell, 1891.

Trench, Richard C. *Notes on the Parables of Our Lord.* Westwood, N.J.: Revell, 1948.

Vos, Howard F. *The Life of Our Lord.* Chicago: Moody, 1958.